THE EPISCOPAL LEADERSHIP ROLE IN UNITED METHODISM

THE EPISCOPAL LEADERSHIP ROLE IN UNITED METHODISM

ROY H. SHORT

Abingdon Press
Nashville

The Episcopal Leadership Role in United Methodism

Copyright © 1985 by Abingdon Press

All rights reserved.
No part of this book may be reproduced in any manner whatsoever without written permission of the publisher except brief quotations embodied in critical articles or reviews. For information address Abingdon Press, Nashville, Tennessee.

Library of Congress Cataloging in Publication Data

Short, Roy H. (Roy Hunter), 1902-
  The episcopal leadership role in United Methodism.

  1. Methodist Church—Bishops. 2. United Methodist Church (U.S.)—Bishops. I. Title.
  BX8345.S47 1985   262'.12   84-28265
  ISBN 0-687-11965-0

ISBN 0-687-11965-0

MANUFACTURED BY THE PARTHENON PRESS AT
NASHVILLE, TENNESSEE, UNITED STATES OF AMERICA

INTRODUCTION

For thirty-six years the writer has been a member of the Council of Bishops, first of the Methodist Church and then of The United Methodist Church. He has watched the bishops come and go during these years, two hundred eighteen in all, ninety-six of whom have finished their course and gone on to their eternal reward.

In the early years of his episcopacy, the writer for the most part sat quietly and observed the other members of the council, often charmed by their insight, creativeness, and dedication, particularly that of some of the more seasoned members. For sixteen years as the secretary of the council he found himself in a position to know more intimately all the members of the council through the contacts and correspondence involved in the nature of that office. In twelve years as a retired bishop he has found great joy in observing the more recently elected episcopal leadership of the church.

The author's *History of the Council of Bishops of the United Methodist Church, 1939-1979* included brief pen portraits of all the bishops of that period whose lives had become a closed book. In this current attempt to comment upon the leadership role of the council, pen portraits are drawn of the bishops who have died since the publication of the previous volume and also of the living bishops of this forty-year period (1939–1979). Some other author some day may be expected to write the story of the additions to the episcopal leadership of the church after 1979.

My thanks to Bishops L. Scott Allen, Ralph T. Alton, Paul W. Milhouse, and W. McFerrin Stowe, the reading committee appointed by the council, and to my wife, Louise, who proofread the manuscript and aided in the research.

Roy H. Short
June 28, 1984

CONTENTS

I.	Episcopal Leadership in United Methodism	9
II.	The Earlier Bishops and Methodist Union	17
III.	The First Leadership Team in The Methodist Church	48
IV.	Additions to the Episcopal Leadership Team, 1940–1967	67
V.	Episcopal Leadership in a Critical Era	144
VI.	New Leadership for a New Church	153
VII.	Additions to the Episcopal Leadership Team, 1972–1976	174
VIII.	Exercising a Group Leadership Role Today	203

I
EPISCOPAL LEADERSHIP IN UNITED METHODISM

The Constitution of The United Methodist Church provides that the Council of Bishops "shall meet at least once a year and plan for the general oversight and promotion of the temporal and spiritual interests of the entire Church and for carrying into effect the rules, regulations and responsibilities prescribed and enjoined by the General Conference" (Par. 52). The fact that this call for episcopal leadership is lodged in the Constitution, which can be changed only by a two-thirds vote in the General Conference and the Annual Conferences, speaks pertinently to how essential the church judges the episcopal leadership role to be.

Such an expectation of episcopal leadership is no new thing. The 1784 Christmas Conference, at which Methodism was organized, wrote into the first *Discipline* of the church the provision that one of the duties of the bishop was "to direct in the spiritual business of the societies." A similar expectation of episcopal leadership has been embodied in one form or another in every Methodist *Discipline* since then. The churches of the Evangelical United Brethren tradition also looked to their bishops for overall leadership, although their concept of the episcopacy differed slightly from the concept obtaining in Methodism.

The *Discipline* in the Constitution calls for leadership upon the part of the Council of Bishops, and the legislative section calls for leadership upon the part of each individual bishop at the point of his or her episcopal area. Numerous specific responsibilities of the bishop are carefully spelled out, all of which taken together mandate the individual bishop to take a positive leadership role, but at the same time this role is to be shared creatively with the district superintendents, the clergy, and the laity of the Annual Conference.

Beyond what, from time to time, has been formalized in the *Discipline,* the expectation of the membership of the church in general is that the bishops individually and collectively shall play a strong leadership role. This expectation is reflected in articles and editorials appearing occasionally in the church press; in periodic pleas from theologians and other church leaders; in actions of the General Conference assigning to the bishops responsibilities in churchwide endeavors; and in the endless correspondence that comes to the desk of every active bishop urging him or her to do something about a particular situation that represents to the writer a matter of serious concern. The expectation sometimes takes the form of criticism, which avers that the bishops are failing to play some anticipated leadership role, and sometimes of encouragement to them to speak on an issue or to act in a certain circumstance.

In the beginning the bishops of the Methodist Church, the United Brethren Church, and the Evangelical Association played a leadership role that was almost all-embracing. In early Methodism Bishop Coke and Bishop Asbury edited the *Discipline,* and apparently by their own action in editing the *Discipline* of 1787 they changed the term *superintendent* to *bishop.* What little publishing was done prior to the establishment of the Publishing House in 1789 seems to have been in the hands of the bishops. After its establishment, they continued for some years to be intimately related to its affairs, even being involved in decisions pertaining to what should be published. The custom followed by the Publishing House today of sending to the bishops copies of its various publications ultimately comes from this situation of long ago.

In 1816 the General Conference authorized the bishop presiding, or a committee appointed by him, to work out a course of reading to be pursued by candidates for the ministry in each Annual Conference. This arrangement remained until 1848. At that General Conference the bishops as a college were authorized to prepare a uniform course of study to be used throughout the church. This responsibility remained theirs until 1916 in the Methodist Episcopal Church and until 1938 in the Methodist Episcopal Church, South.

Like the Methodist Church, the Evangelical and United Brethren churches developed required courses of study for their preachers, and in the earlier days the bishops appear to have had a part in that development and in seeing that the preachers pursued the proper course. In later years, beginning in 1897 in the United Brethren Church, the course of study was closely linked with the seminaries, and the same close relationship obtained in the Evangelical United Brethren Church which in 1946 created a General Commission in Ministerial Training. All bishops of the church were members of the boards of the seminaries and of the various agencies; thus, they had opportunity to offer input on what was to be studied by the preachers. If it is true that what one reads determines largely what one thinks and does, the bishops had by this medium an unusual opportunity to help shape the ministry of the church.

Before the Methodist Missionary Society was established in 1820, the bishops individually and collectively took the lead in the church's first missionary endeavors.

In the early years following the establishment of the Missionary Society by the Methodist Episcopal Church, the bishops took a strong lead in its affairs. An interesting example is found in the case of Bishop Beverly Waugh, who, sitting by his desk before an open window, saw William Taylor passing along the street and said to himself, "I must enlist Brother Taylor." He stepped to the street to stop him and enlist him for an inimitable career in California and a future that included Taylor's establishment of missions on four continents. It was not until 1836 that the Methodist Missionary Society had its first full-time executive in the person of Nathan Bangs, which meant that for the first sixteen years of its existence the bishops of necessity had to take the lead.

The United Brethren Church established a Missionary Society in 1841 and reorganized it in 1853. The Evangelical Church organized a Missionary Society in 1839, and all ministers of the church were automatically members. The Evangelical United Brethren Church, created in 1946, had a Board of Missions with three departments; all bishops were members of the board.

For a century and a half before the Methodist church chose to create a Board of Evangelism, it looked to the bishops to take the lead in evangelism. There was a time when the bishop asked each preacher in open conference, "How many conversions did you have this year?" The Evangelical and United Brethren bishops did the same thing. They were evangelists themselves and felt the obligation to create an evangelistic ministry.

The same evangelistic emphasis marked the episcopacy of the United Brethren Church and the Evangelical Association. The immortal Bishop John Seybert, who traveled 175,000 miles (as recorded in his diary) for twenty years on horseback and for another twenty years in his little one-horse wagon and saw souls converted wherever he went, is an unforgettable example of the evangelism that sustained these two churches for almost two centuries. Bishop Christian Newcomer was the shining example of this evangelistic type in the United Brethren Church.

As the Methodist Episcopal Church grew, the all-encompassing leadership exercised at first by the bishops came by the order of the General Conference to be shared with other persons and agencies. In 1820 the Methodist Missionary Society was created, conceived at the beginning merely as a support agency to which individuals and churches made contributions. This developed soon into an administrative agency. The general secretaryship of the later Board of Missions, in the Methodist Episcopal Church, the Methodist Episcopal Church, South, and the Methodist Protestant Church, was looked upon as a major position in the life of the church and was filled by election by the General Conference. This procedure obtained in these Methodist bodies until 1939 when the board was given the power to elect its executive. The Evangelical United Brethren Church followed the policy of General Conference election to the important post of mission executive until union in 1968.

Some mission executives proved to be remarkably strong persons such as John P. Durbin, Adna W. Leonard, Frank Mason North, and Ralph C. Diffendorfer of the Methodist Episcopal Church; Walter R. Lambuth, W. W. Pinson, and W. G. Cram of the Methodist Episcopal Church, South; George W. Haddaway of the Methodist Protestant Church; and John Schaefer of the Evangelical United Brethren Church. Some of them were dominating personalities who did not hesitate to take issue with bishops if they judged it necessary. One living bishop still keeps in his files a letter from a one-time mission executive who took exception to a move which the bishop made during his first year of attempting to administer one of the mission fields. The letter said, among other things, "Maybe you think you know how to run this work better than we do, but we don't think so."

From 1939 until 1956 all the active bishops in the United States were members of the Board of Missions of The Methodist Church. This was because of the unique administrative character of this board and also because it was believed that the participation of all active bishops would have promotional advantages. Some persons think something has been lost to the church now that all active bishops no longer have contact with an administrative agency whose wide-sweeping field of operation touches in some way the work of every episcopal area in the world. The reduction of episcopal board membership may have been one more indication of a long-prevailing resentment in some quarters to what is often termed *episcopal power*, though it did not appear so at the time, nor was this argument made then. Rather, it was affirmed that the move was made in the interest of efficiency and economy; it reduced the extra area responsibilities for the resident bishop.

The exact relationship between the board as an administrative agency and the bishop as an administrator in a particular area has never been fully spelled out. As a result there sometimes has been misunderstanding between board executives and their staff and the local administering bishop, especially in what were once known as "the overseas mission fields" of the church.

THE EPISCOPAL LEADERSHIP ROLE IN UNITED METHODISM

The original, all-embracing leadership role of the episcopacy in Methodism was affected by the development of other agencies in addition to the first two—the Publishing House and the Missionary Society. These later developed agencies are not administrative in character in the sense that the Board of Global Ministries is, but nevertheless in various ways they do sometimes affect the leadership role of the area bishop. They can, and usually do, play a supportive role to the bishop in his or her administration of the episcopal area. Sometimes, however, they also create problems for the bishop as he or she has to live with the reaction in the churches to some position the agencies have taken or some activity they have sponsored. If monitoring responsibilities are theirs, the bishop is affected helpfully or adversely by the way in which they handle such responsibility. Perhaps church agencies most affect the assigned leadership role of the bishops when, deliberately or unintentionally, they in effect ask the Council of Bishops to become a promotional agency. For the council to exercise the leadership the church expects of it, it must itself be a body which initiates rather than one which merely responds.

Not only has the leadership role played by the episcopacy in earlier years been affected by the development of boards and agencies, but it has also been affected by changes in legislation regarding the episcopacy itself made by successive General Conferences.

The original call of the Methodist Church to the bishops to take leadership was accompanied by the grant of almost unlimited power. But as time has passed, the church has seen fit to abridge this initial grant of power, while still looking to the episcopacy for strong leadership. A good example is the legislation regarding appointment making as it has changed periodically. At one time some bishops went through a somewhat formal consultation with their cabinets, and then they proceeded to make the appointments alone if they saw fit. As late as 1910 provision was written into the *Discipline* of the M.E. Church, South, that the bishops must read the appointments to the cabinet before announcing them. Such solely personal exercise of the episcopal office as once practiced by some bishops belongs to yesterday, but the church today still deems it wise to place careful restrictions upon the exercise of the appointing power. Details with reference to appointment making are now spelled out in the *Discipline* to a degree never obtaining before. Within these limitations the bishop is still charged with the long-term leadership role at the conference level of finally fixing the appointments.

Another change affecting an earlier leadership role played by the bishops in the Methodist Church has been that of removing much of the nominating process from episcopal hands, at both the General Conference and Jurisdictional Conference levels. The same process has been continued at the Annual Conference level by removing much of the nominating responsibility from the hands of the cabinet. The theory behind the former practice of lodging much of the nominating process with the Council of Bishops at the general church level and with the College of Bishops at the jurisdictional level was that in the council or the college every church, every local interest, and every individual Methodist had representation in the person of the area bishop. The same logic obtained in the case of nominations at the conference level by the cabinet where every church and every individual member was represented by some district superintendent.

Now most nominations are lodged with a nominating committee, and some of its members may occasionally represent group interests and pressures. No members necessarily are in position to match the bishops and the district superintendents in their knowledge of the personnel of all the churches.

Methodism has always delighted in tinkering with its machinery, and to some extent it has modified its structure every four years, some General Conferences radically modifying it. A careful study made by Mrs. Faith Richardson, secretary to the secretary of the Council of Bishops, showed that the 1980 General Conference changed 88 percent of Part IV of the 1976 *Discipline*. Quite naturally, because of the nature of the office, the episcopacy has always been a favorite target for modification. The latest attempt in this area came at the General Conference of 1976 when a change from life to term episcopacy was strongly advocated by some persons. The proposed change received a substantial vote.

What the church could have expected in the way of strong episcopal leadership had term episcopacy prevailed is anyone's guess. With <u>an eight-year limit to the office as</u> proposed, the probabilities are that rapid turnover in the council's membership would leave it without continuity and forego the possibility of the type of leadership represented in the past by some of the council's strongest members, such as Bishops Francis J. McConnell, Edwin Holt Hughes, Herbert Welch, James Baker, Arthur J. Moore, John M. Moore, A. Frank Smith, and Paul B. Kern, all of whom held council membership for some years. In the Evangelical United Brethren church Bishops George Epp, Grant Batdorf, Reuben Mueller, Harold Heininger, and John S. Stamm gave similar long years of episcopal leadership. While the move for term episcopacy failed, the provision for an eight-year limit of service upon an episcopal area did prevail. If that is applied rigidly, the eventual effects upon episcopal leadership at the area level remain to be seen.

Despite legislative changes by which the General Conferences from time to time have abridged the episcopacy, the church's expectation for the episcopacy to maintain a strong leadership role continues unabated.

At the area level, each active bishop follows his or her own particular style of leadership. Such styles differ as widely as the respective personalities of the bishops and range all the way from close, intimate, personal attention to details through constant sharing with the cabinet, the Council on Ministries, and task forces to large delegation of responsibility to other parties, such as administrative assistants or office personnel.

II
THE EARLIER BISHOPS AND METHODIST UNION

The story of how the bishops of United Methodism have sought to respond to the mandate to oversee the temporal and spiritual affairs of the church is a long and fascinating one. Many of its most significant chapters are now largely forgotten.

There is no finer example of positive episcopal leadership than in the case of Methodist union in 1939. The union of 1939 is to be credited predominantly to a leadership role played by certain bishops of the Methodist Episcopal Church and the Methodist Episcopal Church, South, and certain presidents of the Methodist Protestant Church.

The detailed story of the steps that led to the 1939 union is told by Bishop John M. Moore in his *Long Road to Methodist Union*. To appreciate fully the episcopacy's role in achieving the union, one must consider certain bishops and their individual contributions.

The story of episcopal leadership in this union actually begins much earlier than 1939 and involves some bishops who are now only dim figures in the long Methodist story.

The Methodist Protestants had withdrawn in 1828 to become an independent body, and the General Conference of 1844 had witnessed the division of the church into the Methodist Episcopal Church and the Methodist Episcopal Church, South. The three churches for almost a century existed as separate entities, often at war with each other, especially preceding and immediately following the Civil War.

The first approach to reconciliation between the churches of the North and the South came in 1869 when Bishop

Edmund S. Janes and Bishop Matthew Simpson visited the College of Bishops of the M. E. Church, South, in session at St. Louis. They carried with them a communication from the bishops of the Methodist Episcopal Church signed by Bishop Thomas A. Morris, president, and Bishop Davis W. Clark, secretary. The communication proposed a canvasing of "the propriety, particularly and methods of reunion." All four of these Methodist Episcopal bishops invite review.

Bishop Morris was the senior bishop of the Methodist Episcopal Church, having been elected in 1836. He was born in what later became West Virginia, and his early ministry was spent in Ohio, Kentucky, and Tennessee. Coming out of border territory he had ties both North and South. During his early years in the episcopacy he had held most of the conferences in the South and had many friends and admirers there. In the General Conference of 1844 he had exerted his best influence to preserve the unity of the church, but his efforts were to no avail. When the die was finally cast, he chose to remain with the Methodist Episcopal Church. A few days after the adjournment of the 1844 General Conference, Bishop Morris was married to his second wife, who was from Louisville. In the hope of being somehow helpful he attended the organizing conference of the M. E. Church, South, in Louisville in 1845 and was invited to share in presiding, but he declined. At one point he participated in a devotional service; otherwise, he remained a spectator.

He afterward noted that his "efforts at friendliness accomplished nothing except to invite suspicion of him in the North." With such a background it was natural that Bishop Morris should desire ardently the reunion of the church. All those individuals who had shared with him in the episcopacy at the time of the 1844 General Conference when the church divided were now deceased except Bishop Andrew of the M. E. Church, South, and Bishop Janes elected at that General Conference. The communication specified Bishop Morris and Bishop Janes as the persons designated to present it, but for some reason Bishop Morris was not able to be at the St. Louis meeting. Bishop Simpson took his place. Perhaps no episcopal leader in the Methodist Episcopal Church would at that time have had larger appeal to the bishops of the M. E. Church, South, than Bishop Morris, for all knew his kind feeling toward the South and his fervent desire for the Methodists to be one people.

The other name signed to the communication was that of Bishop Davis W. Clark, the secretary of the Board of Bishops. This episcopal name could be expected to invite a totally diffent reaction from that to the name of Bishop Morris. Bishop Clark had been elected to the episcopacy in 1864, one of the three "war editors" elected that year, all of whom had campaigned in their columns for the full prosecution of the war and the defeat of the South. Bishop Simpson spoke of him as "a man of decided views and great firmness of purpose." He led the advancement of the Methodist Episcopal Church into the South with the organization of churches and Annual Conferences beginning in 1866. A constituency was found among blacks who had left the M. E. Church, South, among Unionists who had remained with the M. E. Church, South, after the 1844 division, and among Northern people who had newly settled in the South after the war. The South considered this so-called "invasion" under Bishop Clark and others to be unwarranted and a violation of the provisions of the original Plan of Separation. Needless to say, Bishop Clark's signature as secretary added little weight as far as the Southern bishops were concerned.

Bishop Janes, the senior of the two bishops who bore the communication, had been elected by the 1844 General Conference with the strong support of Southern delegates. He was a New Englander by birth and a member of the New York Conference at the time of his election. As financial secretary of the American Bible Society, he had made many friends in the South. Dr. W. W. Capers of South Carolina, in particular, later a bishop in the M. E. Church, South, was his ardent advocate and supporter. When the die finally had to be cast and Bishop Janes chose to remain with the Methodist Episcopal Church, his Southern supporters felt something of a letdown. Yet they understood how natural it was for him to cling to that part of the church in the section from which he came. In the fall of 1844 he held the Kentucky Conference, the

Tennessee Conference, and the Conferences in the Southwest and saw all of them elect delegates to the organizing convention of the M. E. Church, South, due to be held in Louisville in May, 1845. Now after an absence of twenty-five years and at the age of sixty-two, he was once more in the South seeking to heal old wounds and to invite the reunion of the church.

The second Methodist Episcopal bishop sent to St. Louis, Bishop Matthew W. Simpson, was well known by the Southern bishops, although they viewed him somewhat unfavorably. In the General Conference of 1844 he had stood with those who voted, in effect, the suspension of Bishop Andrew, but he had also voted for the Plan of Separation. He had moved the appointment of a committee to reply to the protests of the Southern delegtes to the Andrew decision. In 1845 he had gone to Louisville to witness the proceedings of the organization of the M. E. Church, South, from a seat in the balcony of Fourth Street Church. In the 1848 General Conference of the Methodist Episcopal Church he had been a leading figure in repudiating the Plan of Separation as adopted in 1844. In his arguments on the floor he laid the blame entirely upon the South. He had also advocated refusing to receive Dr. Lovick Pierce, the fraternal messenger sent by the M. E. Church, South. As editor of the Western Churches *Advocate* from 1848 to 1852, he had entered the political arena to espouse views to which many Southerners took strong exception.

He had been elected a bishop in 1852. During the war he had welcomed and acted upon the order of Secretary of War Stanton, turning over to Methodist Episcopal bishops certain Southern Methodist pulpits, in effect making the conquests of the Union armies the conquests of the Methodist Episcopal Church. In contrast to the prevailing Southern contention that the church should stay out of politics, he had been active in them, had been the confidant of presidents, especially of President Lincoln, and had even gone to the point of insisting that Methodists be given post office and other appointments in proportion to the percentage of the population they represented. He had worked closely with the radical

The Earlier Bishops and Methodist Union

Republicans and had advocated the impeachment of President Andrew Johnson. With such a background he was scarcely the best person to send with a message of reconciliation to the bishops of the M. E. Church, South, at that time.

The bishops of the M. E. Church, South, received the deputation and formulated their reply in a written statement signed by Bishops Paine and McTyeire. Now far up in years Bishop Andrew was in St. Louis at the time but did not join the bishops when they met together; his absence was due to feebleness, according to the Southern bishops.

Bishop Paine, who signed the paper as chairman, was the senior active bishop of the M. E. Church, South. He was a Tennessean, elected by the first Southern General Conference in 1846. In the General Conference of 1844 he had been the chairman of the committee that brought in the Plan of Separation. Bishop McTyeire, who signed the paper as secretary, had been a bishop for only three years. He was due to be the dominating figure in Southern Methodism for the next quarter of a century; his primary concern was the building up and strengthening of the church he loved in the section he loved.

The reply of the Southern bishops was courteous but restrained. It spoke candidly of what it considered the offenses of the Methodist Episcopal Church against the Methodist Episcopal Church, South, particularly the refusal to receive Dr. Lovick Pierce as fraternal messenger to the 1848 General Conference, the building of altar against altar in the South under the leadership of Methodist Episcopal bishops, and the seizure of Southern pulpits during the war. The conclusion of the statement was that better fraternal relationships would have to be established before organizational unity could be considered.

Despite the issue of the episcopal conversations in 1869, the Methodist Episcopal Church sent Bishop Janes and Dr. W. L. Harris, later a bishop, to the 1870 General Conference of the M. E. Church, South, in Memphis. Dr. Harris unfortunately spoke of "coming back home." The M. E. Church, South, looked upon the separation of 1844 as an agreed upon division, not as a withdrawal. Dr. John C. Keener, elected bishop at the same conference, took the floor to deliver a stinging rebuke and to advocate vigorously the Southern version of what happened twenty-six years before. Dr. Harris's mistake in inviting the M. E. Church, South, "to come home" was repeated in 1910 when Governor J. Frank Hanley, fraternal delegate of the Methodist Episcopal Church to the General Conference, made a similar remark. Bishop A. W. Wilson who was presiding brusquely turned aside the remark.

At the General Conference of the M. E. Church, South, meeting in Louisville in 1874, the Methodist Episcopal Church again sent representatives. They were Dr. A. S. Hunt, Dr. C. H. Fowler, later elected bishop, and General Clinton B. Fisk. Their approach met with favor, and the ultimate result was a move by both churches toward fraternity rather than union. The M. E. Church, South, in turn sent fraternal messengers to the 1876 Methodist Episcopal General Conference. Both churches appointed commissions to remove obstacles to full fraternity.

The two commissions met at Cape May, New Jersey, in August, 1876, and adopted a formal statement that both churches were legitimate branches of the original Methodist Episcopal Church.

The adoption of this position proved to be a major achievement on the long road to final union. There were no bishops on the Cape May Commission, but Dr. R. K. Hargrove of Tennessee, who later became a bishop, was one of the commissioners of the M. E. Church, South, and Dr. John P. Newman of Washington, D. C., who also later became a bishop, served as one of the commissioners of the Methodist Episcopal Church.

There was to follow a long period of almost twenty years when little more was done until the 1894 General Conference of the M. E. Church, South, appointed a Commission on the Federation of Methodism, and the 1896 Methodist Episcopal Church responded with the appointment of a similar commission. Southern bishops serving on the commission were Bishops Granbery, Hargrove, and Duncan. Methodist

The Earlier Bishops and Methodist Union

Episcopal bishops serving were Bishops Merrill, Ninde, and Fitzgerald. Dr. E. E. Hoss, Dr. R. J. Cooke, and Dr. Luther B. Wilson, all of whom later became bishops, were members. The commission was continued the next two quadrennia, and Bishops A. W. Wilson, Atkins, Walden, and Cranston were added at various times. The commission developed a common catechism, hymnal, and order of worship, and it worked out an arrangement whereby the Methodist Episcopal Church, South, would care for the work in Brazil and Cuba, and the Methodist Episcoal Church the work in Puerto Rico and the Philippines. The Commission on Federation gave way in 1910 to a Federal Council with some increased power to resolve situations.

Several moves were made during the next few years, the detailed story of which does not belong here. They reached their culmination in a Plan of Union adopted by the 1924 General Conference of the Methodist Episcopal Church and by a special session of the General Conference of the Methodist Episcopal Church, South, in July, 1924. The plan failed of final adoption, however, when it did not receive the necessary majority in the Annual Conferences of the M. E. Church, South.

During this long period of moves and countermoves, certain bishops gave devoted and strong leadership to the cause of union. One of these was Bishop Earl Cranston of the Methodist Episcopal Church. Bishop Cranston was a native of Ohio, elected to the episcopacy in 1896. He had been an officer in the Union army, and he was a man of unflagging spirit. As bishop he served the Portland area and the Washington area. He was a persistent and untiring advocate of Methodist union. He took the position that the two divided Methodisms were equally a part of the Methodist Church. He served on all the agencies dealing with attempts at union from 1908 almost to the time of his death in 1932. He was willing to enter freely and candidly into full discussion, and he was able to understand the other person's viewpoint. He was ready to make concessions in the interest of a larger end. He accepted the idea of the jurisdictional system, which proved finally to be the key to union, and it was his suggestion that the black membership of the church be constituted one of the jurisdictions, rather than becoming identified with other black Methodist bodies as some persons on the commission had proposed. Of course, this in effect would have been to invite them out of the church of their fathers. He wept for joy when both General Conferences in 1924 approved a Plan of Union and was greatly disappointed when it failed to win necessary approval in the Annual Conferences of the M. E. Church, South. Bishop Cranston, however, refused to lose heart in the pursuit of his dream of Methodist union, and at seventy-five he wrote *Breaking Down the Walls* in which he sounded once more the call for Methodists to lay aside their differences and become again one people.

Contemporary with Bishop Cranston was Bishop Eugene R. Hendrix of the Methodist Episcopal Church, South. Bishop Hendrix was a native of Missouri who was elected bishop in 1886. He came from a family of means, and married into an affluent family, the Scarritts of Kansas City, Missouri. He had unusual educational advantages for his day, and he received much of his training in the North at Wesleyan College in Connecticut and Union Seminary in New York. He had been recommended for the ministry by the quarterly conference of Washington Square Church, New York. His first pastoral assignment was to a Southern Methodist Church in Kansas, and his other pastoral appointments were to churches in Missouri, a border state. With his background of rewarding contacts in the North during his student days and his experience of unhappy clashes between the two Methodisms in his early ministry, union was quite naturally more appealing to him than to others whose experiences had been different. His basic commitment to union, however, was not because it appeared to be expedient, but rather because he saw it as right.

As early as his twenty-first year, while still in the seminary, he recorded in his diary, "My heart is still set on removing the fierce opposition of the churches along the border." On his thirty-fourth birthday he wrote, "I venture the opinion that 1900 will see but one Episcopal Methodism in this country with three or four jurisdictions."

The Earlier Bishops and Methodist Union

Bishop Hendrix was a courtly man, impressive in his appearance, manner, and dress. He was often affectionately referred to as "Prince Eugene." He continued throughout his long episcopacy the commitment to union. Although he did not serve on committees and commissions to the extent of some of his episcopal colleagues, he consistently threw the weight of his tremendous personal influence in the direction of union. In 1916 he attended the Methodist Episcopal General Conference at Saratoga Springs where he and Bishop Earl Cranston, the two prophets of Methodist union, clasped hands in a dramatic expression of friendship and anticipation of the future. The two bishops maintained a close relationship over the years and kept in continuing correspondence with each other.

Bishop Hendrix never lived to see the realization of his dream. He witnessed with regret the failure of the Plan of Union in 1924 but had gone on to the other world twelve years before Methodist union came at last. In 1939 his desk was transported to the auditorium in Kansas City for the Uniting Conference and was used by the secretary, Dr. Lud H. Estes of the Memphis Conference.

A companion figure to Bishop Cranston and Bishop Hendrix during this period was Dr. Thomas H. Lewis of the Methodist Protestant Church. He was not a bishop, for his church had no bishops, but he was its president for twelve years, from 1916 to 1928. For the last eight of these years he gave full time to the office. He was the president of Western Maryland for thirty-four years and the first president of Westminster Seminary for four years prior to that. Bishop Straughn termed him "the most remarkable man the Methodist Protestant Church has produced." He was a strong preacher who possessed remarkable oratorical gifts.

Like Bishop Cranston and Bishop Hendrix, he was a continuing voice crying for Methodist union. Like them, he lived and labored in a period when attempts at union sometimes gained ground and sometimes lost ground. And like them, he died before seeing his dream come true.

In 1908 as the fraternal messenger of his church to the General Conference of the Methodist Episcopal Church meeting in Baltimore, he brought the General Conference to its feet with shouts and laughter and tears as he pleaded for union. Two years later, at the General Conference of the Methodist Episcopal Church, South, meeting at Asheville, North Carolina, he repeated his Baltimore performance.

Between 1910 and 1912 representatives of the three churches held various meetings in which Dr. Lewis participated. From those meetings came suggestions to the three churches as to what union might possibly require. He himself suggested that a plan of union should include (1) a balance of lay and clerical representation in the General and the Annual Conferences, (2) election of district superintendents by the Annual Conferences, (3) a plan for reviewing the appointments, and (4) election of local church officers by the entire membership of the congregation. All this was in line with the policy of the Methodist Protestant Church. He accepted the position that episcopacy should be a feature of the polity of a united church.

At one time during the conversations when the going became rough and positions rigid, and it appeared matters could not be worked out, *Zion's Herald* of Boston came out with an editorial entitled "It's Time to Quit." Dr. Lewis replied in the columns of the same paper a few weeks later with his article entitled "It's Time to Begin."

The 1912 Methodist Episcopal Church General Conference received a report on the conversations during this period in which Dr. Lewis had been so active a participant, but it took no action. The 1914 General Conference of the Methodist Episcopal Church, South, meeting in Oklahoma City also received a report on the conversations and approved them "as tentative but nevertheless containing the basic principles of a genuine unification of the Methodist bodies in the United States." It favored the unification of the Methodist Episcopal Church and the Methodist Episcopal Church, South, in line with these general principles and appointed certain persons to act as commissioners should the 1916 Methodist Episcopal General Conference agree to proceed further. That General Conference responded favorably and once again efforts at union were under way; but while much was gained in reaching possible guidelines for union, union itself could not be accomplished in this period.

For some reason the Methodist Protestant Church was not included in these efforts. Bishop Straughn stated that he was never able to receive a satisfactory explanation for its exclusion. Dr. Lewis watched the efforts of the other two Methodisms to get together until this death in 1929. He was remembered at the Uniting Conference in 1939 as one of the six heroes of Methodist union, and his conspicuous contribution was recalled with utmost gratitude.

A new chapter began after the meeting of the 1934 General Conference of the M. E. Church, South, in Jackson, Mississippi. The Episcopal Address prepared and delivered by Bishop John M. Moore called for moving toward union, and the General Conference approved the appointment of a Commission on Union. The 1932 General Conference of the Methodist Episcopal Church had already appointed such a commission, as had the 1932 General Conference of the Methodist Protestant Church. The Joint Comission began meeting in August, 1934, and by August, 1935, had ready a Plan of Union to submit to the churches.

The contribution of the bishops serving on the Joint Commission was outstanding. Bishop William F. McDowell served as joint chairman from the Methodist Episcopal Church. He was the senior bishop of that church at the time, a man of striking appearance who was committed to the devout life, a tremendous preacher, and a leader greatly loved throughout the entire connection. Elected to the episcopacy in 1904 he had served the Chicago and the Washington areas. He was fully dedicated to the achievement of Methodist union and served on every commission attempting to deal with that subject from 1916 to his death. After Bishop Cranston's death in 1932, Bishop McDowell succeeded him in the chairmanship of the Methodist Episcopal commission. Bishop John Moore said of him that he was not creative in devising provisions of the plan but that his mental alertness, generous spirit, great heart, and devout approach to problems represented a most significant leadership contribution. The finest example of this leadership probably came at a meeting of the Joint

Commission at Louisville in 1935. One night it seemed that a hopeless impasse had been reached over the question of what was to be the place of the black membership in the new church. Bishop Hughes said that Bishop McDowell went to his room with a drawn and quivering face but returned the next morning with an illuminated countenance. He had spent most of the night in agonizing prayer, and at five o'clock in the morning an idea flashed upon his mind which he interpreted as guidance. He sketched hastily certain legislative changes which were accepted by Bishop Mouzon and his colleagues from the M. E. Church, South, and the crisis was resolved.

Bishop McDowell reached retirement in 1932; nevertheless, the Methodist Episcopal Church continued him as the head of its commission, and in this capacity he labored untiringly.

He lived to see the completion of the Plan of Union, to present it to the 1936 General Conference, and to witness its adoption there. He did not live to see the consummation of the union for which he had labored so long, for he died suddenly in April, 1937. Like Bishops Cranston and Hendrix and Dr. Lewis he was remembered at the Uniting Conference as one of the six heroes of Methodist union.

Bishop McDowell was succeeded by Bishop Edwin Holt Hughes as the chairman of the Methodist Episcopal section of the Joint Commission. Bishop Hughes had been a bishop since 1908 and had served the San Francisco, the Boston, and the Chicago areas. When he assumed the chairmanship, he was serving the Washington area, where his friend and predecessor, Bishop McDowell, lived in retirement. Bishop Hughes had served on the commission which brought in the previous Plan of Union that failed adoption in 1924. The 1932 General Conference appointed him to the new Joint Commission on Union. When the Joint Commission got under way in August, 1934, he was made a member of a smaller committee of eighteen charged to lay the groundwork for the future tasks of the commission. The bishop was not the church lawyer type, but his profound gift of insight enabled him to make invaluable contributions to the proceedings. The entire commission profited by his humor, brotherliness, and openness of heart and mind.

Bishop Hughes was above all else the evangelist of Methodist union. He took the platform in its behalf, not only in his own church but also in the Methodist Protestant Church and the Methodist Episcopal Church, South. He was one of the strongest preachers Methodism has had in the twentieth century. His presentations were so engaging and so winsome that he made friends for union wherever he went. In his appearances in the South he often broke down resistance by the magnetism of his personality and the persuasiveness of this appeal.

At the Uniting Conference it was natural that he should be chosen to bring the closing message on the unforgettable night when Methodist union at last became a reality. It was a deeply moving address, and one of the wonders of it was he had only three days' notice that he would be the one called upon to speak in that memorable hour. As the evening came to its closing moments, Bishop John M. Moore, who was presiding, surrendered the chair to Bishop Hughes to close the conference.

Bishop Hughes lived to see one year of service in the Washington area and ten years as a retired bishop of the new church. He attended the meetings of the council with regularity, often taking the floor to express his thoughts on whatever was before the body. He took particular interest in, and had a kind word especially for, the young bishops who had been chosen to pick up responsibility where he and others had had to lay it down.

The head of the Methodist Protestant commission of the Joint Commission on Union was Dr. John C. Broomfield, the president of the Methodist Protestant Church at the time. He had long been a leader among Methodist Protestants and had served as president of the Pittsburgh Conference from 1924 to 1929. He was elected president of the Methodist Protestant General Conference in 1928 and served until 1936. Bishop John Moore stated that he made most valuable contributions to the proceedings of the Joint Commission in its sessions between 1934 and 1936. Under the Plan of Union the Methodist

Protestant delegates at the Uniting Conference were authorized to elect two bishops, and one of the two elected was Dr. Broomfield, although at the time he was already sixty-seven years of age. The election was a high tribute to the regard in which he was held by his church. He was assigned to the St. Louis area, where he served for four years until his retirement. Bishop Broomfield was primarily a preacher and an evangelist of power. He continued in retirement his effective proclamation of the good news until his death in 1950.

In 1936 Dr. Broomfield was succeeded as president of the Methodist Protestant Church and as head of the Methodist Protestant section of the Joint Commission by Dr. James H. Straughn. At the time much of the work of the commission had already been done, and the Plan of Union was ready for submission to the 1936 General Conference of the Methodist Episcopal Church and the Methodist Protestant Church. What remained after adoption by these two General Conferences was the vote in the Annual Conferences of the two churches, then consideration of the Plan of Union by the M. E. Church, South, and finally the Uniting Conference. Dr. Straughn found himself a part of all these highly dramatic activities.

He took a positive lead as the Annual Conferences of the Methodist Protestant Church made their decisions. There were strong pockets of opposition to union and genuine fears of being lost in a larger ecclesiastical body. It is to be doubted that the necessary vote in the Annual Conference of the Methodist Protestant Church could have been obtained apart from the personal influence of Dr. Straughn. In this period he also appeared at the General Conference of the M. E. Church, South, in Birmingham, Alabama, to lift a strong and persuasive voice for union.

At the Uniting Conference Dr. Straughn was one of the two bishops elected by the Methodist Protestant delegates. He was assigned to the Northeastern Jurisdiction and set aside for special service helping Methodist Protestant churches and people adjust to a situation in which all their Annual Conferences were to be absorbed into other Annual Conferences, often finding themselves divided between several different ones. Bishop Wallace Brown of the Portland area was the first active bishop of the new church to pass away, and upon his death in November, 1939, Bishop Straughn took over the Portland area. He then served the Pittsburgh area from 1940 to his retirement in 1948.

The bishop found retirement lonely and difficult to adjust to. Most of all he suffered certain disillusionment as he thought he saw his beloved Methodist Protestant element sunk almost without trace in the new larger church. In his retirement he wrote *Inside Methodist Union* which offers valuable insights into the intricacies of the union from the viewpoint of one who was on the inside of the developments that finally made it a reality.

The chairman of the Commission on Union of the Methodist Episcopal Church, South, was Bishop Edwin D. Mouzon. He was a giant of a man physically, mentally, and spiritually. His presence was particularly commanding as he stood straight and tall with serious mien and moved with deliberation and dignity. He was a native of South Carolina and a graduate of Wofford College. He represented the fourth generation of a family of South Carolina preachers. In 1889 he went to Texas, and he spent all his ministry in that state with the exception of a three-year pastorate in Kansas City until his election to the episcopacy. He was a geniune scholar and the only bishop of the M. E. Church, South, to deliver the Lyman Beecher Lectures at Yale which he did in 1929 under the title, "The Program of Jesus."

Bishop Mouzon was elected by the 1910 General Conference of the M. E. Church, South. He was a liberal compared to most bishops of the southern church at that period. It was the period of the Vanderbilt controversy that resulted eventually in the loss of the school by the church in 1914, and he found himself a somewhat lonely figure in the College of Bishops in that era when feeling was so intense, for he did not agree with the position of most of the bishops on the Vanderbilt issue. His loneliness in the college began to change with the election of Bishop John M. Moore in 1918.

Throughout his episcopacy Bishop Mouzon was committed to Methodist union. He served on every commission of the

M. E. Church, South, dealing with union from 1916 onward. Bishop John Moore said of him, "No man was his superior in advocating union." When union failed in 1924, he wrote to Bishop Earl Cranston, "We will not stop . . . so long as I live I shall plead the cause."

In 1930 he had his chance to help reopen the matter as he was the bishop chosen to deliver the Episcopal Address to the General Conference of the M. E. Church, South. In it he included a vigorous plea for further union negotiations.

During the processes that finally resulted in the perfection of a Plan of Union between 1934 and 1935, Bishop Mouzon along with Bishop McDowell and Dr. Broomfield carried a heavy burden of responsibility.

It was the lot of Bishop Mouzon, like Moses, to climb the mountain and look over into the Promised Land but not to enter in himself. He died suddenly on February 10, 1937, when the Methodist Episcopal Church and the Methodist Protestant Church General Conferences had already acted but the vote in the General Conference and in the Annual Conferences of his beloved M. E. Church, South, lay some months in the future.

Upon the death of Bishop Mouzon, Bishop John M. Moore took his place as chairman of the commission of the Methodist Episcopal Church, South. The two were striking contrasts physically, since Bishop Mouzon was unusually tall and broad shouldered and Bishop Moore was rather short. But they were much alike in their thinking and commitments and were close friends.

Bishop Moore was an exceptionally well-educated man for his day in the church; he held a doctorate from Yale and had studied at Leipzig and Heidelberg. As a young preacher he had held distinguished pastorates in Texas and Missouri, and from 1910 to 1918 he was the secretary for Home Missions of the M. E. Church, South. In 1918 he was elected to the episcopacy, representing what most of the then older bishops looked upon as a too liberal type.

His interest in Methodist unification traced as far back as his student days at Yale where he was ordained deacon by Bishop Fowler of the Methodist Episcopal Church. At Yale he also met for the first time Bishop Charles B. Galloway of the M. E. Church, South, who said to him, "It does seem the North and the South could find some way of uniting." This occasion was the beginning of a friendship with Bishop Galloway that grew with the years.

As early as 1911 Bishop Moore (not yet a bishop) appeared in print as an advocate of Methodist union. At that time he wrote an article for the *Christian Advocate* which suggested that the merged church have a new name, be composed of a General Conference and Regional Conferences, and that all black Methodists unite in a single body.

Bishop Moore served on the commission that produced the Plan of Union rejected in 1924 and the one that produced the plan accepted in 1939. His services on the commission were most important. He always did his homework and never went to a meeting unprepared. Again and again he would draw from his pocket a carefully thought-out proposal to be accepted, amended, or rejected. He had peculiar gifts of insight, and often when it seemed an impasse had been reached, he would suggest a way through it. Because of his habits and gifts he was often named to subcommittees set up to address a particular problem.

Bishop Moore was truly a little giant. He was a very firm man, and once he arrived at a position he tenaciously held to it. On the other hand he had due respect for the opinions of others, and where he concluded adjustment was necessary he made adjustment. His approach to the major problems of union was by way of constitutional provision. In the early days of the Prohibition amendment there was a little song often sung by the Women's Christian Temperance Union ladies that had in it the line, "It is in the constitution and it's there to stay." Bishop Moore felt the same way about what he had helped to write into the constitution of the united church. Had he lived he would probably have been surprised at the constitutional changes coming to a head in 1968 and some attempted constitutional changes in the General Conference of 1976.

Another example of Bishop Moore's firmness was his strong adherence to the idea of the "ordination" rather than the "consecration" of bishops. In his *Life and I* he said, "I was ordained, not consecrated a bishop," and in his *Long Road to Methodist Union* he spoke of the ordination not the consecration of the Methodist Protestant bishops at the Uniting Conference.

Bishop Moore played the pilot role in the last General Conference of the M. E. Church, South, held in 1938 at Birmingham. He retired from the active episcopacy that year but was chosen to devote the entire following year to promoting Methodist union and to making ready for the Uniting Conference.

It is noteworthy that eventual changes in the commission's leadership from the three churches meant that the three chairmen who gave final leadership to the perfection of union were all born in border states, Bishop Hughes in West Virginia, Bishop Moore in Kentucky, and Bishop Straughn in Maryland. In the border states the tragedy of Methodist division had been experienced most acutely.

Thus far we have dealt with the four bishops and the two Methodist Protestant presidents who were chairmen of the respective commissions whose work culminated in the union of 1939. But other bishops, who as working members of the commissions made significant contributions, also deserve mention.

One of these was Bishop Frederick D. Leete. Bishop John Moore spoke of him as "one of the most valuable members of the Joint Commission." Elected a bishop in 1912 he served on every commission on union from 1916 on. His first episcopal assignment was to the Atlanta area of the Methodist Episcopal Church, composed of white and black conferences in Georgia, Alabama, Florida, and South Carolina. He was the first resident Methodist Episcopal bishop in Atlanta for twenty-eight years since the residency of Bishop Warren. He served the Atlanta area for eight years, grew well acquainted with the leaders of the M. E. Church, South, came to understand the southern mind, and made it a policy to seek to create mutual understanding in various ways. No Methodist Episcopal bishop serving on the commission had lived more intimately with the situation of three historically related churches operating in the same territory, often with unhappy rivalry, than had he.

Bishop Leete was a rather crusty individual who sometimes bluntly expressed himself. Both Bishop McDowell and Bishop Hughes praised his ability for succinct statements. He was a matter-of-fact person, well informed in church law. His approach to union was a practical one. He felt that union ought to occur, and he was willing to give and take toward the accomplishment of what he conceived to be so desirable an end.

He was a great admirer of Bishop John Moore and gave him much credit for the achievement of union. In his autobiography *The Adventures of a Traveling Preacher,* Bishop Leete wrote, "My own effort, with few addresses in the Joint Commission, was to make parliamentary motions in harmony with Bishop Moore's leading, and in our own Commission to answer questions and remove misunderstandings."

After serving the Atlanta area, Bishop Leete served in turn the Indianapolis and the Omaha areas. He retired in 1936 as the movement for union was reaching its final stages. He was present at the Uniting Conference as a retired bishop and participated in its proceedings. It represented for him the realization of a long-cherished hope.

Another bishop who made significant contributions to the achievement of union is Bishop Edgar Blake. Bishop John Moore termed him "the most creative and efficient member of the Commission."

As far back as 1916, Bishop Blake had been a member of the commissions of the Methodist Episcopal Church working on union. He was at the time the corresponding secretary of the General Sunday School Board. At a working conference held in Evanston in February, 1916, at which thirty-four papers were presented, he read a paper in which he strongly favored Regional or Jurisdictional Conferences and also a Judicial Council. Bishop Moore claimed that Dr. Blake's paper laid the base for what eventually developed. At the working conference Bishop Moore also presented a paper advocating the same things.

Bishop Blake, like Bishop John M. Moore, was a short

man. He had a particularly incisive mind and a gift for analysis. He was inclined to speak up readily and to enter fully into whatever topic of discussion was before the house.

These earlier attempts at union in which Dr. Blake participated did not come to realization. In 1920 he was elected to the episcopacy and assigned to the Paris area where he served eight years, returning to the States in 1928 to serve first the Indianapolis and then the Detroit areas. He was not a part of the commission that formulated the Plan of Union rejected in 1924 or of the new commission set up in the thirties. When Bishop McDowell died in 1937, Bishop Blake was named as his replacement on the commission. Thus the gifted bishop credited with having done so much to help lay the early foundations for union participated once again in the final stages of its accomplishment.

Two other Methodist Episcopal bishops served on the commission which saw union become a reality—Bishop Robert E. Jones and Bishop E. G. Richardson. Bishop Jones, like Bishop Leete and Bishop McDowell, served on all the commissions dealing with union, beginning in 1916. In his first days of service he was not a bishop but the editor of the *Southwestern Christian Advocate*. In 1920 he was elected to the episcopacy along with Bishop M. W. Clair, Sr., the first black to be elected general superintendent in the Methodist Episcopal Church. He was throughout his life a strong defender of the interests of his people. Bishop John Moore said that in the union discussions he confined himself largely to provisions regarding the black membership.

Bishop Richardson served on the commission from 1928. He had a good legal mind but does not appear to have been able to devote as much time to the Joint Commission as some of his episcopal colleagues due to heavy episcopal responsibilities in Puerto Rico. He was quite active, however, in the preparation of the prospectus for the proposed *Discipline* of the new church.

Another Methodist Episcopal member of the Joint Commission who made invaluable contributions was Dr. Willis J. King. Five years after union he was elected to the episcopacy and served with distinction in Liberia, Louisiana, Texas, and Mississippi.

Three other bishops of the M. E. Church, South, served on the final Joint Commission—Bishops W. N. Ainsworth, Paul B. Kern, and Arthur J. Moore.

Bishop Ainsworth was a tall, dignified, courtly southern gentleman. He was an active and committed member of the Joint Commission. He is generally credited with having been the author of the suggestion that Kansas and Nebraska be placed in the South Central Jurisdiction, an idea that proved helpful as the Joint Commission struggled with the problem of boundaries to ensure jurisdictions of fairly comparable size. Bishop Ainsworth was retired at the 1938 General Conference of the M. E. Church, South. Because of ill health he was unable to attend this General Conference or the Uniting Conference to witness the final consummation of the efforts in which he had participated so faithfully.

Bishop Moore and Bishop Kern were both church statesmen. Bishop Hughes praised them as invaluable counselors, particularly at the point of missionary organization. Bishop Kern had served for four years in the Orient in his beginning episcopacy, and Bishop Moore at the time of his appointment to the commission had just been given the entire mission work of the M. E. Church, South, except Cuba.

Five of the ministerial members of the commission of the Methodist Episcopal Church, South, appointed by the 1934 General Conference were elected as bishops in 1938. They were Bishops Selecman, Holt, Purcell, Decell, and Peele. Bishop Decell was one of the secretaries of the Joint Commission. All had only one year of service as bishops of the M. E. Church, South, and spent the remainder of their careers as bishops of The Methodist Church.

The task of the Joint Commission which saw union realized, like that of the commissions before it, was no easy assignment. There were radically differing viewpoints regarding certain features of polity obtaining in the three churches seeking union. There were also deep-rooted sectional prejudices to be considered. There was the record of a century of operating apart from each other, often in strong competition with each other. And there were some longstanding unhappy memories that refused to die.

Numerous problems had to be dealt with, but the most difficult could be reduced to a few specific ones. One problem involved determining the character of the General Conference. Generally the Methodist Episcopal Church had thought in terms of an all-powerful General Conference, while the southern church had for years thought a General Conference should be subject to some limitations. At the time of the division in 1844 the occasion had been the slavery question, brought to a head in the case of Bishop Andrew. But accompanying that issue was a sharp division of opinion among the delegates relative to the power of the General Conference. The Plan of Union carefully spelled out that the General Conference was to have full legislative power over all matters distinctively connectional subject to a vote in the Annual Conferences on constitutional matters.

Another issue concerned adequate protection for the interests of all segments of a world church. This was taken into account in the Plan of Union's provision for Jurisdictional and Central Conferences, with the election of bishops lodged in such regional conferences. Thus every section of the church was guaranteed a continuing representation in the episcopacy that could not have been guaranteed by the election of bishops in a large General Conference. However, there was nothing to prevent a jurisdiction's going outside its bounds to elect a bishop, and that is exactly what the Central Jurisdiction did in the case of Bishop Lorenzo King and the Western in the case of Bishop Kennedy. The Jurisdictional and Central Conferences provision further assured the representation of all sections of the church in the membership of general boards and agencies.

Numerous persons in the northern section had serious misgivings about the jurisdictional system aside from their objection to the provision for a Central Jurisdiction based upon race. Some regarded it as a possible fifth wheel. Others objected to it because it took the election of bishops out of the General Conference. Bishop Leete spoke for many persons, however, when he wrote in his *Adventures of a Traveling Preacher,*

> The old General Conference of the Methodist Episcopal Church, after the fiasco of the Des Moines session of 1920, was a body that I was not loath to see replaced by the present Jurisdictional Conference system. The new plan has its perils . . . but it is not subject to the positive evils of the old General Conference of the larger group in Methodism.

Another problem was that of the laity's place in the new church. Here the position of the Methodist Protestant Church was adopted: every charge was to be represented by a lay delegate in the Annual Conference, and an equal number of clerical and lay delegates was to attend the General, Jurisdictional, and Central Conferences.

The episcopacy posed another problem. Here the general pattern followed in the Methodist Episcopal Church and the Methodist Episcopal Church, South, was adopted, and the Methodist Protestants who did not have bishops went along with this position.

The question of where to lodge the final interpretation of the law was answered by The Plan of Union, which followed the example set by the M. E. Church, South, during the previous quadrennium in its establishment of a Judicial Council. Up to this point, all three churches had been dissatisfied with other solutions to this issue.

Perhaps the most sensitive question concerned what to do about the black conferences that had been a part of the life of the Methodist Episcopal Church for three quarters of a century. The Methodist Episcopal Church, South, had organized its black membership into an independent church in 1870, with which it had maintained a supporting relationship. In 1939 racial prejudice had not abated to the extent it has today, although much of it still remains to be overcome. Its presence was a factor in the achievement of union.

The members of the Methodist Episcopal commissions felt a deep loyalty to the black conferences and cherished their long and significant ministry. Eventually the Joint Commission recommended the establishment of a Central Jurisdiction composed of the black conferences. No one perhaps stated the thinking of much of the North at this point more effectively than did Bishop Hughes. He said, "The Methodist Episcopal Church had separate Negro churches, separate Negro Conferences, separate Negro Areas, a separate Negro Advocate, and two bishops elected on separate ballot from which white ministers were excluded. These conditions had prevailed among us and had excited little controversy. Could we now demand that the union should go beyond what we ourselves had accepted?"

According to Bishop Hughes, some of the strong black leadership of the church at that time, such as Matthew S. Davage, W. A. C. Hughes, Edgar Love, and Willis King, agreed to the plan of a Central Jurisdiction. Also friends of the blacks saw in it a possible advantage for the black membership. Bishop Thirkield had given much of his life to black higher education, and as a bishop he had held most of the black conferences. He wrote, "The proposed plan of unification offers to our Negro membership the broadest and most inclusive national Methodist Episcopal Church fellowship, the greatest opportunity for effective interracial contacts and activities and the chance for permanent and effective leadership." Bishop McConnell, while not entirely happy with this feature of the plan, observed, "The proposals do give the Negro more than he has had and make it possible for him to take still more."

The Central Jurisdiction did represent an effective power base for the black membership of the church. In thirty years, however, the church became convinced that racism should not be structured in its life, and when The United Methodist Church came into being in 1968, there was no provision for a Central Jurisdiction.

The episcopal leadership given in developing the Plan of Union was supplemented by certain members of the commission who were not bishops, especially Dr. Thomas D. Ellis of the South Georgia Conference of the M. E. Church, South; Dr. F. W. Mueller, Dr. James R. Joy, and Dr. Harry Woolever of the Methodist Episcopal Church; and Dr. A. Norman Ward of the Methodist Protestant Church. Dr. Ward died before the work of the commission was completed and was remembered at the Uniting Conference as one of the heroes of Methodist union. Coming from a church with no episcopacy and agreeing that the new church should have bishops, he would take the floor in opposition whenever a proposal was made to weaken the episcopacy, insisting that the only episcopacy worth having was a strong one.

Some casual espiscopal conversations that ultimately contributed to union should be noted. So often, when the full story is known, informal meetings and contacts and behind the scenes of formal events have helped to pave the way. One such event occurred in 1929 when Dr. Hawley and Dr. Allen called at the office of Bishop Welch, then the resident bishop of the Pittsburgh area, to talk about the Methodist Protestants coming as a body into the Methodist Episcopal Church. Bishop Welch relayed the conversation to Bishop McDowell who came to Pittsburgh in January, 1930. A luncheon meeting was arranged, and Bishop McDowell, Bishop Welch, Dr. Hawley, Dr. Allen, and Dr. Broomfield attended. The whole affair was informal and unauthorized, but it served to reopen the issue of union. The group agreed that the Methodist Episcopal Church, South, should be involved also if it could be arranged.

Another informal conference which bore much fruit was one held in Atlanta in October, 1931, during the Methodist Ecumenical Conference. At that time Bishops McDowell, Welch, Meade, and Leete, and Dr. Broomfield met with Bishop John M. Moore to discuss what could be done to reopen the question of union which had bogged down a few years before.

These two instances suggest something regarding the leadership often taken by bishops not only in conferences, commissions, and committees but also in informal ways. How much additional light would be shed upon the history of United Methodism if somehow the story could be known of the countless informal conversations of its episcopal leaders as they have faced together the concerns of the church.

With the Plan of Union finally developed, the first body to deal with it was the General Conference of the Methodist

Episcopal Church which met in Columbus, Ohio, in 1936. There the debate centered chiefly around the provision of the plan for a jurisdiction based upon race. The opposition to such a provision was led largely by Dr. L. O. Hartman, editor of *Zion's Herald,* elected to the episcopacy in 1944; by Dr. Ernest Freemont Little; and by Dr. David Jones, a black leader from North Carolina and a brother of Bishop Robert E. Jones. The final approving vote in the General Conference was 470 to 83. In the succeeding Annual Conferences the vote consisted of yeas 17,239, nays 1,862.

In the Methodist Protestant General Conference the margin of victory was 142–39. The negative vote was due more to a conservatism that feared union with what it regarded as a too liberal church than to objections to the plan itself. Twenty of the twenty-five conferences of the Methodist Protestant Church voted for union and five against it. The Annual Conference membership vote was comprised of 1,265 in favor and 389 against.

The vote in the M. E. Church, South, was taken first in the Annual Conferences. The tabulation showed 7,650 favorable votes and 1,247 opposing ones. This meant that the last step remaining for approval of the plan was the vote of the General Conference of the M. E. Church, South.

The General Conference met in Birmingham, Alabama, in May, 1938. Other issues were before the conference, but the overriding issue was that of Methodist union. Bishop Edwin Holt Hughes and Dr. James H. Straughn (later bishop), the chairmen of the Methodist Episcopal and Methodist Protestant commissions, were both present and addressed the conference in moving messages. Bishop Leete, long active in union commissions, and Bishop Flint of the Atlanta Area were present as visitors as were a number of connectional officers of the Methodist Episcopal Church.

One could see throughout the conference the steady, quiet, guiding hand of Bishop John M. Moore bringing the ship at last into port. This was supplemented by the superb floor leadership of Dr. T. D. Ellis of South Georgia who had had so much to do with the development of the plan. The strategy was to let those persons opposed have the floor as much as they desired. Nothing was to be done to cut short debate. One speech followed another, many of them not too impressive, until at last it was concluded by both sides that the time had come to vote. The vote was taken by roll call, and the plan was approved by a vote of 434 to 26. Only five clerical votes in the entire General Conference were cast against its adoption.

So that everything might be in due order, the College of Bishops then proceeded to ask that the Judicial Council rule upon the legality of the action taken. The Judicial Council invited appearances from any concerned parties. Taking leadership in challenging the legality of the action was Bishop Collins Denny, four years retired and one of the greatest legal minds southern Methodism ever had. He not only appeared with his son, a lawyer from Richmond, before the Judicial council, but he also worked the halls and the hotel lobbies interviewing delegates before the vote was taken. His contention before the Judicial Council was that the vote in the Annual Conferences had failed because all the Annual Conferences had not approved it; therefore, the General Conference had no authority to proceed to vote in the matter. In only one Annual Conference, the North Mississippi, did the plan fail to receive a majority vote, and there it failed with 117 yeas against 125 nays.

The Judicial Council in an extended opinion ruled that what was required for passage was a majority of the votes cast in all the Annual Conferences, rather than a majority vote in each particular Annual Conference. Had this been true, a few votes in one smaller Annual Conference could have defeated the will of several thousand other Methodists as expressed in their vote.

Bishop Denny appeared for his last time at the General Conference at Birmingham. Through the years he had served on several bodies dealing with union, but he could never agree with the idea. He had too many memories of the aftermath of the Civil War and of Reconstruction days to be able to change. He was an unforgettable figure at Birmingham, a noble old warrior fighting his last battle for the southern church to which he had given his life and now losing that last battle.

Of the delegates at Birmingham in 1938, seven were elected

to the episcopacy that year: Bishops Holt, Peele, Purcell, Decell, Selecman, William C. Martin, and Watkins.

Three others were elected in 1944: W. Angie Smith, Paul E. Martin, and Paul N. Garber. Two others were elected in 1948: Marvin A. Franklin and Roy H. Short. Nolan B. Harmon was elected in 1956. Cyrus B. Dawsey, a delegate, was elected a bishop of the Brazil Methodist Church in 1946.

It may be asked why union was at last approved by such a large vote in all three churches. There were, of course, a variety of reasons. The primary reason was that most of the generations with memories of the Civil War and Reconstruction had passed away. Another reason was that both the Methodist Episcopal Church and the Methodist Episcopal Church, South, had long since accepted the Methodist Protestant position on laity rights, which to a great extent had been the occasion of that particular division. Again, a new leadership had arisen in all the churches willing to go beyond where some of the former leadership could agree to go. The strain of the depression years clarified the idea that competition among churches of the same heritage was not only wasteful and foolish but also wrong. Beyond all else the churches moved toward union because of a growing sentiment that it was the right thing to do.

With the approval of union by the General Conference of the M. E. Church, South, all necessary preliminary steps had been taken. The next year was spent in getting ready for the Uniting Conference.

Much of the year was spent in perfecting a prospectus of a *Discipline* for the new church. A provision in the Plan of Union stated, "The legislative power of the Uniting Conference shall be confined to harmonizing and combinng provisions now existing in the Disciplines of the three churches or one or more of these churches." This was a protective measure and left new changes in legislation to the 1940 and succeeding General Conferences. The Uniting Conference therefore was more like a constitutional convention than a regular General Conference. It did receive a limited number of petitions—slightly less than four hundred—which were referred to the respective committees, but none involving proposed legislation that was not in any one of the three *Disciplines* could be handled. A number of bishops served on the eight subcommittees dealing with the sections of the prospectus. These were: Conferences; Ministry and Judicial Administration; Membership and Temporal Economy; Missions; Education; Publishing Interests; Superannuate Support; and Rituals and Orders of Worship. Particular leadership in preparing the prospectus was given by such bishops as John M. Moore, James H. Straughn, E. G. Richardson, and W. W. Peele. The prospectus was mailed to the delegates a month prior to the Uniting Conference.

The long years of attempting to achieve Methodist union reached their climax with the Uniting Conference at Kansas City, April 26 to May 10, 1939. The guiding hand of Bishop John M. Moore was felt throughout the conference, and the strong influence of Bishop Hughes and President Straughn was also apparent. All the bishops, except a few detained because of age or illness, were on the platform, and all participated in one role or another.

Much of the time of the conference was spent in perfecting the initial *Discipline* of the new church. This was an attempted harmonization of the *Disciplines* of the three uniting churches, which did not involve too difficult a task. Despite their separate existence for a century, the three churches had much legislation in common. It is interesting to note in the present day when women have become so much a part of the ministry of the church, including the district superintendency and the episcopacy, that a minority report was presented at the Uniting Conference providing that "women are included in all provisions both for the local and for the traveling ministry." The minority report failed adoption by only thirteen votes; the final count was 384 to 371. One of the signers of the minority report was Dr. Fred G. Holloway, who was elected bishop in 1960. The Methodist Protestant Church to which he belonged did admit women into the ministry.

Another responsibility of the Uniting Conference was the assignment of the bishops to jurisdictions and residences. The Plan of Union provided that the Uniting Conference should do this but did not specify how to accomplish this task. The result was a good deal of maneuvering and debate in which there were moves and countermoves. There was a proposal to put the matter in the hands of a special committee elected by the delegates, but finally the responsibility was lodged with the legislative Committee on the Ministry which in the debate had taken the position that the assignment was its logical responsibility.

Another responsibility of the Uniting Conference was to solve the matter of overlapping boundaries of the conference of the three churches. Meetings of the delegates from the respective jurisdictions recommended what the new conference boundaries within the jurisdiction should be.

Still another concern for the Uniting Conference was the merger of the various boards and agencies and their future location. This was approached by the appointment of a special committee to report to the 1940 General Conference.

The highlights of the Uniting Conference were certain great hours, which now have their permanent place in the memories of the church. Among those were the communion service for delegates only, held in the Episcopal cathedral, and the opening session of the General Conference in the auditorium to which the bishops and delegates had marched in procession from the church. There were the flare of trumpets, the inspiration of great music, the strong Episcopal Address by Bishop John Moore, and the deep emotion felt by the delegates as they sat down together to close the book on a century of division and bring into being once again a united church.

Another highlight of the conference was the consecration of the newly elected Methodist Protestant bishops, J. H. Straughn and J. C. Broomfield, held on Sunday afternoon, April 30, with the consecration sermon being brought by Bishop Adna W. Leonard.

The most unforgettable occasion of all was the final night, Wednesday, May 10, 1939, with Bishop John Moore presiding and Bishop Hughes bringing the address. As the service drew to its close, Bishop Moore put the final vote on the Declaration of Union, inviting the bishops also to join in the standing vote, although technically they had no vote. The vote was unanimous. It was 9:12 p.m. The long efforts of so many bishops and others to bring into being a united church had at last borne fruit, and it was appropriate that Bishop John L. Nuelsen, who was the attending bishop of longest standing, should give the closing benediction.

III
THE FIRST LEADERSHIP TEAM IN THE METHODIST CHURCH

In the first forty years of the life of the Council of Bishops following its organization in 1939, a total of 223 persons constituted its membership. Eighteen of these were already in retirement at the time the council was formed. All the others served at least one episcopal area of the Methodist Church or The United Methodist Church.

The majority of the bishops in the forty years of the council's history have functioned primarily at the level of the area to which assigned. It is to the area that most bishops have devoted their time, attention, and energies. Twice a year the area bishop has gone to the meetings of the Council of Bishops to consider the concerns of the total church.

The bishops of the church have been and continue to be greatly differing personalities. Some are vocal while others are reticent. Some are incisive in thinking while others lack the gift of analysis. Some give welcome attention to details while others shrink back from what appears to them dull routine. Some relish debate and are quick to take the floor while others hestitate to plunge into discussion and do so only when they feel strongly led. In a body of the nature and size of the council certain persons naturally emerge to play a strong leadership role at both the council and larger church levels.

When the Council of Bishops was born in 1939, some dynamic leaders of the predecessor churches of the council were already in retirement. From the former Methodist Episcopal Church there were such leaders as Bishops Herbert Welch and Frederick D. Leete, and from the former

Methodist Episcopal Church, South, came Bishop John M. Moore. At the 1940 Jurisdictional Conferences one year later, they were joined by Bishops Edwin Holt Hughes, Edgar Blake, Charles Mead, and John L. Nuelsen, and five years later by Bishop Francis J. McConnell. All these retired bishops enjoyed participating in the discussions of the council, and the council valued the accumulated wisdom which their years of experience represented.

With such former episcopal leaders no longer on the active list, it became incumbent upon the Council of Bishops of the new church to develop new leadership, and this it was not long in doing.

G. BROMLEY OXNAM

Doubtless the first significant step in the developing of leadership for the new Council of Bishops was the election in 1940 of Bishop G. Bromley Oxnam as secretary. For the next sixteen years he, more than any other person, was to determine the character of the operation of the council. The presidents of the council were elected for one year and then gave way to someone else, but Bishop Oxnam remained at his post. He was an assertive personality, firm in convictions, creative in mind, incisive in understanding, and gifted in the ability to get things done. He was a master of detail and wrote shorthand, which stood him in good stead as a secretary. By the sheer strength of his personality, whether consciously or unconsciously, he converted the secretaryship into the "driver's seat" of the council. He himself made the agenda after requesting by mail items that members of the body might desire listed for consideration. He would also find ways and means to list some items that he thought merited the attention of the council, but ones that no bishops had sent in. At times he would do this by introducing some communication he had received personally from some source, rather than as secretary of the council. The president, in the days of Bishop Oxnam's secretaryship, was the presiding officer, but the secretary was really the pilot of the ship.

The bishops had great confidence in Bishop Oxnam and

great respect for his judgment. Most of them, including the ones who served as president, were quite content for him to carry the council.

He insisted that all meetings of the council be strictly executive. In taking this position he was holding to a long-time precedent for the meetings of the bishops of both the Methodist Episcopal Church and the Methodist Episcopal Church, South. In order that necessary information might be available to the press, he would have one of the bishops named as press representative to report through a Methodist Information representative to the church and secular press. He was against having outsiders address the council except in rare instances. He took the position that when a church agency had something to say to the bishops, it was best for it to be said through one of the bishops serving on the board of that agency. He sought to encourage the bishops to think through matters for themselves and to play the leadership role the church expected of them. He objected vehemently to other agencies of the church calling meetings either before or after the council meeting in the city where the council was convened.

Bishop Oxnam was all-business, and he wanted the council to be that way, too. He gave "every passing moment something to keep in store" and thought everybody else should do the same thing. He kept the council on its toes, insisted that a close schedule be followed, and was impatient with any wasting of time by some talkative brother that he judged to be long on discourse and short on ideas. Before Bishop Oxnam's secretaryship, the meetings of the bishops apparently had followed a rather loose pattern of procedure, but he converted them into meetings which were fully business and such they have remained ever since.

It is disturbing to realize that prior to Bishop Oxnam's day, minutes of the meetings of the bishops were kept by the secretary and sometimes shared in duplicate form with the members of the council, but there seemed to be no official depository. Most minutes of the Board of Bishops of the Methodist Episcopal Church and of the College of Bishops of the Methodist Episcopal Church, South, are now lost.

Random copies occasionally turn up among the papers of some deceased bishop or are discovered in some long-overlooked hiding place.

Bishop Oxnam not only took leadership for sixteen years in perfecting the mechanics of the operation of the council and in keeping it running smoothly, but he also took marked leadership in promoting various causes which had appeal to his reason, his conscience, and his heart.

No member of the Council of Bishops was more committed to ecumenism than was Bishop Oxnam. He was an energetic advocate of the National Council of Churches and the World Council of Churches, and no American Methodist of his time exercised more leadership within these organizations than he did. He served from 1944 to 1946 as president of the Federal Council of Churches, and he was a member of the presidium of the World Council of Churches from 1948 to 1954. He endeavored to keep the necessity of ecumenical cooperation in the thinking of his fellow bishops and saw to it that matters related thereto were often on the agenda of the council. The executives of the World Council and the National Council valued his judgment, as did ecumenical leaders all over the world. Both organizations profited by his power of analysis, his creative imagination, and his ability to get things done.

Another cause to which Bishop Oxnam was devoted was peace. While World War II was still going on, he was among the creative spirits planning for a just and durable peace. He sought to commit the council and the church to this objective. In February, 1943, he led thirty-two bishops in a visit to President Roosevelt, Vice-President Wallace, and members of the cabinet and of the Supreme Court to call to their attention the necessity of achieving a just and lasting peace. He was the father of the Crusade for World Order, approved by the Council of Bishops and by the 1944 General Conference. Under Bishop Oxnam's leadership a series of small study books on world order was developed and used extensively throughout the church.

Bishop Oxnam was interested in the worldwide operation of the church. For four years he was the chairman of the World Division of the Board of Missions. He traveled extensively and knew firsthand the church overseas from the United States. It was his conviction that every bishop needed not only to know his own area but also to be familiar, to some extent at least, with the wider expanse of Methodism. Before the rise of the Central Conference system, most of the bishops, especially in their beginning episcopacy, had seen service in some episcopal area overseas, but the day had come by the time of Methodist union that almost no bishop in the States had served overseas. Accordingly, Bishop Oxnam gave to the church another of his brain children, what was originally known as the "plan of overseas visitation," under which each effective jurisdictional bishop would make each quadrennium a visit of some length to some area of the work of the church overseas from the United States. The plan has proved of inestimable value and is still in operation. It has been extended to include visits by Central Conference bishops to other fields.

There is yet one more cause cherished by this bishop which should be mentioned. Bishop Oxnam came into the episcopacy from the educational world, as the president of DePauw University, and his concern for Christian higher education never abated. It took its most concrete form in the perfection, under his guidance, of a new relationship of American University with the Methodist Church and in the establishment of Wesley Seminary in the nation's capital.

Bishop Oxnam was ingenious in getting done whatever he set out to do. He used to say, "Where is the point of decision? Get to that point." And he himself seemed always to know unfailingly where the point of decision was and how to get there.

ARTHUR J. MOORE

Another strong leader in the Council of Bishops, beginning with its organization in 1939 and continuing for the next twenty years, was Bishop Arthur J. Moore, who came out of the Methodist Episcopal Church, South. In his beginning ministry Bishop Moore had been a professional evangelist. Following a brief career in this field, he became in turn the pastor of two great churches—Travis Park, San Antonio, Texas, and First Church, Birmingham, Alabama. In these great pulpits he remained the evangelist, preaching to capacity crowds every Sunday. In 1930 he was elected to the episcopacy at the age of forty-two.

Bishop Moore had a great commitment to missions, and he came to be regarded as one of the great missionary statesmen of the church. As a young preacher he had applied for missionary service but was turned down by authorities at that time. His first episcopal assignment was to the work of the Methodist Episcopal Church, South, on the West Coast, all of which was small and widely scattered. In 1934, at the bottom of the depression, the Methodist Episcopal Church, South, found itself under the necessity of serious retrenchment. It recalled to service in the United States three bishops who had been serving overseas and gave all the mission work of the church, with the exception of Cuba, to Bishop Moore. This meant that he had at one time responsibility for the work in China, Korea, Japan, Africa, Belgium, Poland, and Czechoslovakia. For five years he shuttled back and forth across this vast expanse of earth, in a day when intercontinental air travel belonged to the future.

With the organization of the new church, Bishop Moore was elected president of the Board of Missions and continued in this office for twenty years until his retirement in 1960. He was no mere presiding officer of the board, but rather an active, aggressive, assertive leader who insisted upon being a full party to all decisions. He masterminded the consolidation of the foreign work, the home work, the women's work, and the church extension work of the three uniting churches. He worked with some forceful personalities, such as Dr. Ralph Diffendorfer of the Foreign Division; Dr. E. D. Kohlstedt of the Home Division; Dr. T. D. Ellis and Dr. Frederick W. Mueller of the Church Extension Section; and Mrs. J. D. Bragg of the Women's Society of Christian Service. But Bishop Moore remained in full control of the ship at that time and for the next twenty years as other leadership developed and as issues changed. He was an unusually gifted, assertive person, and without seeking to do so, by the sheer strength of his personality he dominated almost any situation in which he found himself. His gifts and interests made him a natural leader for the board, and to thousands of Methodists around the world for a quarter century he was "Mr. Missions."

Bishop Moore not only took leadership in missions as president of the Board of Missions but also exercised strong personal leadership as he traveled the world for twenty-five years. He used to assert that he could find himself without a hotel room in almost any great city of the globe and be able to call up someone he knew and find welcome lodgment in a private home. He was a familiar figure on almost every mission field of the church. Strange to say, the one mission field he never visited was the one nearest his Georgia home, Cuba. Perhaps he put off going to Cuba because it was so near home that he felt he could go there anytime. Or maybe he felt no call to Cuba because he thought that world issues found no such focus in the Caribbean island as they did elsewhere. The crisis in Cuba and Cuba's movement onto the stage of international affairs did not come until about the time of his retirement.

In the Council of Bishops, Bishop Moore was a voice forever advocating missions, lifting up mission needs, explaining mission strategy, and sharing mission problems. He was in the council a heart beating with love for all the world and constantly sharing its passion with his episcopal colleagues. He was a soul enthralled with the dream of the coming kingdom and fully confident that ultimately the kingdoms of this world shall become the kingdoms of our Lord and of his Christ.

Because of Bishop Moore's strong commitment to missions, the Council of Bishops called upon him for special services to an extent that it did not call upon any other bishop. When Bishop Garber took over the Richmond area in 1951, following the illness of Bishop Peele, the Council of Bishops assigned the vacant Geneva area to Bishop Moore. When Bishop Ralph A. Ward died, the council asked Bishop Moore to take over the Hong Kong area for a year. When Central Conference sessions were to be presided over until a bishop could be elected, the council called upon Bishop Moore again and again. When emergency situations arose in Africa, India, Malaysia, Hong Kong, or Europe and there was a call for a bishop to give counsel, most frequently the council called upon Bishop Moore. Actually in his heart he welcomed these assignments though they involved lengthy journeys and long absences from home. He would sometimes feign a reluctance to take another such assignment, but actually he was like an ancient fire horse always waiting to be on the way to one more fire.

Strange to say, Bishop Moore was not an active participant in the World Council of Churches or the World Methodist Council. He was fully sympathetic with their work, but his attention and energies were absorbed in the worldwide program of the Methodist Church itself. He devoted himself to this venture and to his area comprised of his native state of Georgia, whose happy episcopal leader he was for twenty years.

Shortly before Bishop Moore died, he wrote his autobiography which was published by Abingdon. It is a brief book which, while beautifully written in his inimitable style, fails to do full justice to so towering a figure in the life of the church. It is interesting to note that he chose as its title, *Bishop to All Peoples*. This is indeed what he was, a fervent spirit whose love knew no bounds and who coveted every little child and every eager youth and the last man or woman in earth's remotest corner for his Lord.

A. FRANK SMITH

Bishop Moore took leadership in the total field of missions, particularly world missions, and Bishop A. Frank Smith of Texas took leadership in home missions, as the national work was called. The two men were bosom friends. As young preachers, both served in San Antonio, Texas—Bishop Moore at Travis Park (the downtown church) and Bishop Smith at Laurel Heights (a suburban church). Bishop Moore used to tease Bishop Smith, saying that people went to Laurel Heights on Sunday morning to hear Dr. Smith brag on what saints they were and then to Travis Park on Sunday night to hear him tell them what sinners they were. The two were elected bishops at the 1930 General Conference of the Methodist Episcopal Church, South, and both retired in 1960. Just as Bishop Moore was president of the Board of Missions for twenty years, so Bishop Smith was chairman of the National Division for the same period. The division covered a wide spectrum of activities, including the work in Alaska, Puerto Rico, and Hawaii, and a diverse program in the continental United States including work with various minorities, service institutions, rural work, church extension, and pastoral support for new or weak local churches.

Bishop Smith was fully conversant with each feature of the program. The administrators of the division looked to him for counsel and highly valued his wisdom and insights. As an area administrator he knew firsthand that phase of the National Division program represented by the work among the Indians in Oklahoma and among the Mexican Americans in Texas and New Mexico. He brought regularly to the attention of the Council of Bishops the concerns of the National Division, and all the bishops administering in the United States often had occasion to be in contact with him and the Home Division staff regarding situations where the work of the division touched their particular episcopal areas.

HERBERT WELCH

Another bishop taking leadership in the earlier years of the Council of Bishops was Bishop Herbert Welch. For a long period he was the senior member of the council in age. His erect carriage, alert mind, rare wisdom, calm spirit, rich philosophy of life, and happy sense of humor were all undiminished by the lateness of his years. He became in many respects the Nestor of the council, and when he took the floor, the members would respond with high appreciation to his observations as a tried and greatly loved senior statesman of the church. Bishop Welch was already retired when union came in 1939. He had been elected in 1916, and all his active episcopal service had been spent in the Orient except for four years in the Pittsburgh area. After retirement he had served the Boston area for a year following the death of Bishop Burns.

Bishop Welch played one of the most significant roles of his long career after retirement, when he took leadership in the establishment of the Methodist Committee on Overseas Relief. This agency came into being as a result of the concern of the Council of Bishops during and after World War II for the thousands of persons in many lands who were hungry, homeless, dislocated, or otherwise suffering as a result of the war. Bishop Welch at the age of seventy-eight was called to direct the agency, and he devoted eight magnificent years to it. He perfected its pattern of organization and succeeded in laying its objectives upon the heart of the church. The continuing and now vastly expanded ministry of the United Methodist Committee on Overseas Relief still bears the stamp of his leadership of forty years ago.

After retiring from this assignment, Bishop Welch continued active and alert beyond the century mark, and he finished his earthly course at the age of 106.

CHARLES C. SELECMAN

The Board of Evangelism of the Methodist Episcopal Church, South, was established one year before Methodist union out of the 1938 General Conference's conviction that the church needed a fresh emphasis upon evangelism. The Uniting Conference incorporated the Board of Evangelism into the structure of the new church. Dr. Harry Denman was elected the general secretary and Bishop Charles C. Selecman the president of the Board.

Bishop Selecman was a dynamic leader in evangelism throughout his active episcopal career and was the board's president for eight years. He had been a university president at the time of his election. Throughout his ministerial life he remained an evangelist. He was a warmhearted, moving preacher whose sermons were marked by a strong hortatory note. He not only presided over the meetings of the board but also traveled throughout the land participating in evangelistic rallies, institutes, training schools, and other meetings sponsored by the board.

Under a provision then in the *Discipline,* he presented a

report for the board at each meeting of the council. This Disciplinary provision meant that at least some consideration of evangelism was automatically on the agenda of every meeting of the council, and Bishop Selecman made full use of the opportunity afforded by it. He was forever carrying a banner for evangelism and urging his companion bishops to follow suit.

He worked closely with Dr. Harry Denman, whose warm heart and fertile mind were always suggesting new evangelistic endeavors for the church. Together they saw Methodism come to a new effectiveness in seizing evangelistic opportunities. They witnessed the church registering regular gains in membership instead of the large losses that occurred later.

Bishop Selecman was followed in the presidency of the Board of Evangelism by Bishop Ralph Cushman, who was succeeded by Bishop W. Angie Smith. Bishop Smith served in this office for twelve years, until 1964. His leadership was comparable to that of Bishop Selecman. Bishop Smith was followed in the presidency by Bishop Gerald H. Kennedy. Next Bishop Noah W. Moore, Jr., served in that position until his retirement in 1972, at which time the Board of Evangelism was surplanted by a unit in the new Board of Discipleship.

J. RALPH MAGEE

Bishop J. Ralph Magee did not play a large leadership role in the Council of Bishops, although he participated regularly in its discussions and for one year was its president. He confined himself generally to the administration of his area. But there was one significant churchwide project to which he gave distinguishing and long-to-be-remembered leadership. This was the Crusade for Christ authorized by the 1944 General Conference. World War II was drawing toward its close, and the crusade was the church's effort to prepare for the days that lay immediately ahead. The crusade involved (1) the raising of $25 million for postwar reconstruction and mission, (2) a year of emphasis upon evangelism, (3) a year of emphasis upon stewardship, and (4) a year of emphasis upon church school enrollment and attendance.

Bishop Magee was called upon to be the director of the crusade, and to it he devoted four years of vigorous, unwearying leadership. He secured the services of Dr. J. Manning Potts as associate director and of other staff personnel. He enlisted the services of all the related boards and agencies of the church, particularly at the point where their own ongoing program meshed with the objectives of the crusade.

The crusade was launched at a conference of all the bishops and district superintendents of the church, held in Centenary Church, St. Louis, in the fall of 1944.

Under the leadership of Bishop Magee, all the objectives of the crusade were reached. The sum of $27 million rather than $25 million was raised. The Year of Evangelism saw over a million persons added to the membership rolls of the church. The Year of Stewardship saw an increase in total giving and twelve thousand commitments to full-time Christian service. And the Year of Church School Emphasis witnessed an increase in enrollment and attendance in all divisions of the church school.

The crusade, largely due to Bishop Magee's efforts, wrote one of the great chapters in Methodist history and remains in the memory of many as his enduring monument.

PAUL B. KERN

Bishop Paul B. Kern was another episcopal leader who after union gave significant leadership in the Council of Bishops and in the life of the church-at-large at several points. He was an idea man, with an incisive and creative mind. One of his lifetime interests was Christian education through both the local church and institutions of higher learning. As a young minister he had attracted attention throughout the Methodist Episcopal Church, South, by his activities in Epworth League work. For eleven years he had taught at Southern Methodist University, and for six years of that time he was the dean of the Theological School. His active interest in Christian education prompted him to take leadership in the consolidation of the Sunday School Board, the Epworth

League Board, and the Board of Education (Higher) into a single Board of Education by the 1930 General Conference of the Methodist Episcopal Church, South.

During his years as bishop in Nashville, Bishop Kern had his office in the same building with the Board of Education of the new Methodist Church, and the staff turned often to him for counsel. It is appropriate that one of the buildings of the Board of Discipleship in Nashville should carry his name, for no bishop made greater contribution to both the local church section and the section of higher education than did he. For fourteen years he served as president of the Board of Trustees of Scarritt College and left upon that institution an indelible mark.

Bishop Kern had a love for and an interest in young people, and the youth of the church had no greater friend among the bishops of his day. A significant project involving youth to be credited to his imaginative leadership was the Youth Caravan Movement of a half century ago. Under this movement, selected young people were trained together at a center and then deployed as teams into local churches for service during the summer. They received no compensation except room and board. The result was an enriching experience for hundreds of local churches as well as for the young Caravaners themselves. There are many leaders in United Methodism today who got their start in fuller participation in the life of the church in the Youth Caravan Movement.

Bishop Kern also took decisive leadership in the development of the Advance for Christ and His Church, though leadership here was shared with his close friend Bishop Costen J. Harrell. Once the Advance was organized, Bishop Harrell became its chairman. The Advance included two features, the cultivation of Advance Specials by local churches and individuals for particular projects both at home and abroad, and an annual Week of Dedication offering which went each year to the completion of selected building projects, mostly overseas from the United States. The Week of Dedication feature was dropped in time, but the Advance program still continues as one of the primary sources of support for the far-flung activities of the church. For this proven and essential feature of its financial structure, United Methodism remains permanently indebted to Bishops Kern and Harrell.

JAMES C. BAKER

Bishop James C. Baker was another earlier member of the council who attained wide leadership not only in Methodism but also in the ecumenical church. He was an ecumenist ahead of the day when ecumenism became popular, and he was an active participant in the great ecumenical conferences at Oxford, Madras, and Whitby. He was a lively force in the founding of the World Council of Churches, and he was a member of the Central Committee from 1948 to 1954. He was president of the International Missionary Council from 1941 to 1947. His own episcopal career had begun with a period of service as bishop in Japan, Korea, and Manchuria, and his missionary interest continued throughout his life. He helped found the International Christian University in Japan after World War II.

Bishop Baker's lifelong interest was Methodist student work on state college and university campuses. He was himself the founder of the first Wesley Foundation, and his initial interest in student work never abated throughout his life. He knew the student mind and kept abreast of the changes that marked it. In 1956, at the request of the Council of bishops, Bishop Baker wrote a small book entitled *The First Wesley Foundation—An Adventure in Christian Higher Education.* A modest amount of autobiographical material is in it, but that could not have been otherwise, for the Wesley Foundation movement is still the continuing shadow of Bishop Baker. No episcopal leader of the church has deserved more the appellation "The Friend of Students" under his picture in the *Daily Christian Advocate* for the day in 1928 when he first presided in a General Conference.

IVAN LEE HOLT

Bishop Ivan Lee Holt was another member of the Council of Bishops at the time of its organization whose leadership in several areas became widely recognized. One of Bishop Holt's chief interests was worship. He loved liturgy, and from long years of study he became familiar with worship as practiced in various traditions. He was a master of diction, and any worship service he developed bore the touch of a skilled hand. He had a rich mellow voice and a commanding presence. The dignity with which he conducted a worship service was most impressive.

As a young minister teaching at Southern Methodist University, he had shocked the older generation of Texas Methodists as he introduced the use of robes in chapel services and thereby planted in their hearts the fear of Methodism's going formal. As pastor of elite St. John's Church in St. Louis, he made full use of his worship skills and when he entered the ranks of the episcopacy, he did no less. He knew how to give the right touch to an ordination or communion service or even a short devotional period that made them unforgettable occasions. It was natural that he should be among those chosen to constitute the committee that developed the 1935 edition of the Hymnal.

Bishop Holt is to be regarded as a pioneer in the emphasis upon worship which has marked Methodism and United Methodism in more recent years. He was the chairman of the Commission on Ritual and Orders of Worship appointed by the 1940 General Conference which produced in 1945 *The Book of Worship*. He was succeeded in episcopal leadership in the field of worship by Bishop Edwin E. Voight, who in turn was followed by Bishop Lance Webb.

Another field in which Bishop Holt took leadership was ecumenical affairs. He was president of the Federal Council of Churches from 1935 to 1936 and was a delegate to the assemblies of the World Council of Churches at Amsterdam and Evanston. He was a member of the first Central Committee of the World Council of Churches. He was also an early advocate of church union, beyond union within denominational families. In 1946 he was one of the proponents of what was called the Greenwich Plan—a plan which would have looked in time to a merger involving nine denominations. He was elected chairman of the group. To his great disappointment, the proposal proved to be short-lived. Bishop Holt's other major interest was the World Methodist Council of which he served as president from 1951 to 1956.

J. WASKOM PICKETT

Bishop J. Waskom Pickett was the last bishop elected in the Methodist Episcopal Church prior to Methodist union in 1939. He was elected by the Southern Asia Central Conference in 1935 and was forty-five years old at the time. He was to survive all the Methodist Episcopal bishops living at the time of union. He was one of the last missionaries to be elected a Central Conference bishop, and he outlived the other members of that noble company, except Bishops Dodge, Lundy, and Andreassen.

Prior to his election Bishop Pickett had been a missionary in India for many years and had attracted widespread attention by his participation in mass movement evangelism that brought thousands into the kingdom.

Bishop Pickett's father was a nationally known holiness evangelist remembered for the ardor of his preaching, and the bishop had about him something of his father's fire though he did not accept entirely his father's theology. His mother, Ludie Day Pickett, was a woman of unusual gifts and deep conviction who was for years the highly respected president of the Kentucky WCTU (Women's Christian Temperance Union). She was active not only in the WCTU and in church affairs but also in political affairs, particularly in the 1928 election which saw the defeat of the wet candidate, Al Smith. The Pickett family lived at Wilmore, Kentucky, and had close connections with Asbury College and Asbury Seminary. The bishop, like his contemporary and close friend, Stanley Jones, was imbibed with the Asbury spirit, but like Dr. Jones he did not follow the Asbury pattern of thinking completely. He did not hesitate to voice a criticism at any point he thought that pattern proved defective.

Following his election, Bishop Pickett served the Bombay area and later the Delhi area until his retirement in 1956. Mrs. Pickett was the daughter of Bishop J. W. Robinson elected in

1912 and long a leading figure in the life of the Methodist Church in India.

Bishop Pickett was a short, wiry, active man who moved with dispatch. He kept constantly alert to national and international affairs. He had a deep sense of righteous indignation at social wrongs, which often compelled him to speak up. As he bespoke his indignations, his face would flush, his eyes would flash, and his words would pour forth in a hot torrent. His voice had a huskiness that increased its appeal.

At the time Bishop Pickett was elected, Central Conference bishops had certain limitations upon them, such as not being allowed to preside in a General Conference or to have their expenses paid to all sessions of the Council of Bishops. The bishop battled for full Central Conference episcopal participation, and he was the first Central Conference bishop to preside in a General Conference, this call coming to him in 1956. The full participation enjoyed by Central Conference bishops today is probably to be credited to him more than to any other individual.

Following retirement, Bishop Pickett continued preaching, teaching at Boston University, writing several books as well as many articles for the church press, and serving on special assignment by the Board of Missions and other church agencies. In his later days Bishop and Mrs. Pickett made their home in Columbus, Ohio, where he died in 1981.

WILLIAM C. MARTIN

Bishop William C. Martin was elected by the last General Conference of the Methodist Episcopal Church, South, in 1938 from the pastorate of First Church, Dallas. Previously he had served pastorates in Arkansas and Texas. The M. E. Church, South, had not elected any bishops in 1934 because of its difficult financial situation resulting from the depression. Rather it had closed ranks, combined episcopal areas, and increased the work load of all effective bishops. In 1938 with the retirements of Bishops John Moore, W. N. Ainsworth, Sam Hay, H. A. Boaz, and James Cannon, Jr., only five bishops were available for active duty. The M. E. Church,

The First Leadership Team in the Methodist Church

South, decided therefore to elect seven bishops, and Bishop Martin was the sixth of these. Earlier in the balloting Bishop Charles C. Selecman had been elected from the North Texas Conference, the same conference to which Bishop Martin belonged. For two bishops to be elected from the same conference at the same General Conference was unusual.

Bishop Martin saw only one year of service as a bishop of the Methodist Episcopal Church, South, his assignment being to the church's small but by no means insignificant work in California, Arizona, the Pacific Northwest, and Montana. At the Uniting Conference he was assigned to the Omaha area. The next year, following the retirement of Bishop Mead, he took the work in Kansas also. He then served the Dallas area until his retirement in 1964.

William C. Martin was in every respect a quality bishop. Physically he looked the part with his fine build and trim figure. His abstemious habits and his custom of taking long, brisk, daily walks contributed to his excellent health.

He was not a preacher who appealed particularly to the emotions, but he forcefully delivered messages that always had solid substance. He studied assiduously and wrote out carefully what he had to say, and he apparently committed much of it to memory. A striking example of this ability came in 1964 at Pittsburgh where he delivered the Episcopal Address. He read it until he came to its climax; then he laid his manuscript aside and delivered the remainder from memory.

Bishop Martin was greatly interested in every phase of the church's life and was forever probing, asking questions and voicing his concern over issues he felt demanded attention. He was a bishop with the heart of a pastor, and the preachers and lay people of the areas he served knew well that they were constantly in his thoughts and prayers. He was a good administrator, poised and controlled, who paid careful attention to details. His major interests included stewardship, church development, and ecumenical affairs. He was the president of the National Council of Churches for a term, and from 1960 to 1964 he was the president of the World Division of the Board of Missions. For a period he served on the Central Committee of the World Council of Churches.

Bishop Martin participated actively in the Council of Bishops and was its president from 1953 to 1954. The council gave him many responsibilities, some of them difficult, which he dispatched with alacrity and efficiency. He entered fully into floor discussions in the council and made genuine contributions there.

No bishop in his day commanded greater respect than did Bishop William C. Martin. He was known and loved for what he represented. He was the soul of integrity, and everyone who knew him believed him incapable of doing anything little or unworthy. His indignation at wrong was deep but controlled and therefore all the more forceful. His poise, balance, and genuine friendliness were inspirations to his episcopal colleagues.

Upon retiring the Martins continued to live in Dallas where for four years the bishop acted as bishop in residence at Perkins School of Theology. Later they moved to Little Rock, Arkansas, where the bishop had been pastor of First Church in his earlier ministry.

At this writing Bishop Martin continues the lone survivor of the bishops of the Uniting Conference of 1939.

IV
ADDITIONS TO THE EPISCOPAL LEADERSHIP TEAM, 1940–1967

The Jurisdictional and Central Conferences each quadrennium beginning in 1940 added to the episcopal leadership of the church as vacancies in the ranks occurred due to retirement or death. The phrase used originally in Methodism to suggest to the General Conference the election of one or more new bishops was "to strengthen the episcopacy." It is to be hoped that this is what the election of new bishops actually does.

SHOT K. MONDOL

Bishop Shot K. Mondol was elected by the Central Conference of Southern Asia in 1940, after he had served for some years as pastor and district superintendent. He was only forty-four years of age at the time. He was the second native of India to be elected a bishop in the Methodist Church; the first was Bishop Chitambar, who was elected in 1930 and died in 1940. Upon his election Bishop Mondol was assigned to the Hyderabad area, where he served for sixteen years. Following that he served the Delhi area until his retirement in 1965.

Bishop Mondol has soft but penetrating eyes, which have a decided light in them. He is soft-spoken, deliberate in speech, and quiet in manner. He is friendly and cordial in spirit, and he has a good sense of humor.

The bishop knows well the art of public relations and how to cultivate friends. Wherever he went he made friends for India, particularly for projects for which he had administrative responsibility. He did not hesitate to ask for funds from those who had funds to give, and he was adroit in this action. As an administrator he was suave in manner but positive and firm. He was a good preacher, an evangelist at heart, and a reformer with good practical sense and balance. He was highly respected by the political leaders of India to whom he had ready access, and they valued his counsel. Further he had contact across ecumenical lines not only in India but also in the world at large.

Bishop Mondol was for some years, along with the bishops of Singapore and Hong Kong, one of the bishops called upon most frequently to play the role of host. During the years at Delhi he found himself living at one of the crossroads of world travel, and bishops and other church figures were always coming and going. The time was when few bishops of the church had not at one time or another been a guest in his home. Mrs. Mondol had been a missionary and was a daughter of missionary parents; she was well equipped to play the hostess role. The bishop would not only feed and house his guests, but usually he would arrange to take them to a favorite restaurant which specialized in spiced roast chicken and a delightfully good hot Indian bread. He would sometimes arrange interviews for his guests with important national figures, in some cases even the prime minister.

Following retirement, after the Philippines Central Conference in 1965 could not elect a bishop, Bishop Mondol was called upon by the Council of Bishops to care for the vacant Manila area. He and Mrs. Mondol moved to Manila and took up residence in a downtown hotel. Well accepted in the Manila area, they served there until the election of Bishop Guansing in 1967.

Subsequent to the Manila assignment Bishop and Mrs. Mondol moved to Dayton, Ohio. The bishop attended the meetings of the council until the infirmities of age prevented his participation.

FRED PIERCE CORSON

Bishop Fred Pierce Corson was elected in 1944 from the presidency of Dickinson College. He was the first bishop elected by the Northeastern Jurisdiction after the responsibility for the election of bishops was lodged with the jurisdictions. He was assigned to the Philadelphia area following the retirement of Bishop Richardson. At that time the Philadelphia area consisted of the Philadelphia, Wyoming, and New Jersey Conferences and the work in Puerto Rico. In 1964 the New Jersey Conference became the Southern New Jersey Conference and a part of the newly formed New Jersey area.

Bishop Corson served the Philadelphia area throughout his entire active episcopacy until his retirement in 1968. These twenty-four years on the same area are matched in the history of the Methodist Church only by Bishop W. Angie Smith who served exactly the same years on the Oklahoma City area. Bishop Corson was greatly loved in the area, and his return quadrennium after quadrennium was welcomed by many supporters, both clerical and lay. His offices throughout these years were at historic 1701 Arch Street, long the center of the Board of Home Missions of the Methodist Episcopal Church, and later of the Home Division of the Board of Missions of the Methodist Church.

Bishop Corson looked like a bishop. Tall and straight, he carried himself well and was distinguished in appearance. Normally he wore clerical dress and urged his preachers to follow his lead. He had a habit of giving clericals to young preachers and to friends who were not given to clerical attire. He had a wardrobe of robes, hoods, and numerous medals which he would use on state occasions.

He insists upon the importance of the amenities. He cultivated the social graces, and no one is more anxious to do what is proper in every situation than he. He is the embodiment of refinement, understanding, and courtesy.

As an administrator Bishop Corson was careful, methodical, and forthright. He knew personally his churches and preachers, but at the same time he depended upon his superintendents and area assistant. His conference sessions were highlights of inspiration. He made it a practice to bring his brother bishops to them, especially the newer ones, as conference preachers. His ordination services were most impressive and planned with great care. Prior to them he privately lectured the ordinands on certain important matters, one of them usually being ministerial dress. The bishop is fond of young people, and he developed the practice of having young Methodists come to the conference sessions. They came in great numbers, and he always had certain features recognizing their presence.

Bishop Corson assumed quite early a place of leadership in the Council of Bishops. He would take the floor readily on any matter before the council. In 1952, when he had been a member only eight years, he became its president. In 1956, when he had been a member only twelve years, he was chosen to deliver the Episcopal Address. By the time he was half way through his active episcopacy, he already had the highest honors the council can give. The bishops in the southern area of the church found him especially kind and friendly, and he was often in their areas by invitation and they in his. He was particularly close to Bishops Arthur J. Moore, W. Angie Smith, Paul E. Martin, and William R. Cannon.

A friend of the colleges and universities of the church, Bishop Corson emphasized the importance of higher education. From 1948 to 1956 he was president of the Board of Education, and he gave devoted and magnificent leadership. At that time the church thought of the Board of Missions and the Board of Education as the two major boards, and every bishop was on each board. Bishop Corson was close to Dr. John O. Gross, long the church's leader in higher education. The Methodist educational world recognized Bishop Corson for his leadership and writings and often called upon him for lectures and addresses. He received honorary degrees from numerous colleges and universities throughout the land.

Bishop Corson became best known on the world stage for his activities in the World Methodist Council. He became its president in 1961 and served in that office until the election of Bishop Odd Hagen in 1966. He then became an honorary president for life. As president Bishop Corson gave careful attention to every detail of the council's activities. He traveled far and wide to represent the council at important national and international events. Largely under his guidance the World Methodist Council moved from the purely fellowship body that it was for many years to a body having a significantly extensive program operating upon a worldwide basis. Under his leadership the council moved also from a body composed primarily of British Methodists and various brands of American Methodists to a body representing Methodists from all the continents and half a hundred countries.

Bishop Corson urged adequate support for the World Methodist Council. Together with Edwin L. Jones, a layman from North Carolina, and Bishop Paul E. Martin, he secured the strong financial support of the Methodist Church and also helped to develop a program of support involving all the participating Methodist churches.

After Vatican II a new relationship began to develop between the Roman Catholic church and other churches. As president of the World Methodist Council embracing so many various Methodisms, Bishop Corson was one of the Methodist observers. He gave himself with devotion to this assignment and attended all the sessions. A friendship developed between him and Pope John XXIII, and later Pope Paul VI. He had numerous personal interviews with both popes, who highly commended his contributions. Bishop Corson was an ideal person for these Roman Catholic contacts, because in addition to his concern for ecumenical dialogue he had the bearing, the reverence for amenities, and the attachment to formal and symbolic dress which Rome has long associated with the episcopacy.

Long after his retirement Bishop Corson continued his activities in the World Methodist Council, and at its 1981 meeting in Honolulu he was seated regularly on the platform, recognized by all as a father of the council as well as a father in the faith.

When retirement came in 1968, Bishop Corson did not welcome it. Having been at focal points in the life of the church for so long, he did not find it easy to sit back and watch passively. He observed with concern, and sometimes with apprehension, things happening in the life of the church and of the Council of Bishops itself. He would sometimes find himself wanting to step into the fray again.

After retirement Bishop and Mrs. Corson made their home

at Cornwall Manor, Pennsylvania. They continue to spend each winter at St. Petersburg, Florida, where for years they have been among the most distinguished winter colonists.

W. EARL LEDDEN

Bishop W. Earl Ledden was elected by the 1944 Northeastern Jurisdictional Conference from the pastorate of Trinity Church, Albany. Previously he had served strong churches in New Jersey, Rhode Island, and New York. He was assigned to the Syracuse area, which he served until his retirement in 1964.

The bishop is a tall, erect man of fine presence. He has a friendly smile and is known for his warm cordiality. His laugher is infectious and his fine sense of humor never deserts him. In his late days he has had difficulty with both his sight and hearing. One day at the council when he needed to repair his hearing aid and could not see well enough to do it, he made a joke of the matter and said, "Things are getting pretty bad when you can't make your eyes and ears cooperate."

Bishop Ledden is a poet at heart. He has rare good taste in the fields of literature and music that carried over into his preaching. It was reflected dramatically in his worship services which were always works of art.

A master of diction, he carefully chose every word in his sermons. There was a rare beauty about his sermons, and they had a musical quality that was deeply moving.

Bishop Ledden was the musician in the Council of Bishops. He played the piano in the council meetings until he could no longer read the notes because of trouble with his eyes. He stressed, as he had opportunity in the council, the use of the best music and the disuse of hymns he regarded as poor quality. He led in the abandonment of the use of the once popular "bishops' hymn" because he felt it did not measure up to the best musical standards. He had an organ in his home, at which he would spend long, happy hours. Following retirement he spent some years teaching music and worship at Wesley Seminary until the infirmities of age forced him to resign this responsibility. For some unknown reason he was

THE EPISCOPAL LEADERSHIP TEAM 1940–1967

not one of the bishops assigned to the committee which produced the new hymnal in 1964 although he would have been one of the best qualified bishops in the church for that assignment.

Bishop Ledden was greatly interested in all the council affairs, and he participated freely in its discussions. He had a sagacious mind and his insights represented rich contributions. He was a devoted disciple of Bishop Oxnam and trusted in his leadership. He was also a disciple of Bishop McConnell who had profound influence upon him. With two such heroes, he quite naturally took advanced positions on several questions. He was president of the council from 1956 to 1957.

The first Mrs. Ledden, his childhood sweetheart, died in 1957. In 1965 Bishop Ledden married Henrietta Gibson, long the efficient treasurer of the Women's Division of the Board of Missions. The families had been friends for a long time, and it is said that Miss Gibson, held in such wide respect, was most helpful in the election of her pastor in 1944. They became one of the most loved and admired couples in the episcopal family. The Leddens were blessed with resources in excess of those of many episcopal families, and they were continually doing things for others and for good causes. When the council met in Washington in 1973, the Leddens had all the bishops and their wives as personal guests at the Kennedy Center to hear a concert, Mahler's *Resurrection* Symphony. Mrs. Ledden died in 1981. Bishop Ledden made his residence thereafter at Gaithersburg, Maryland.

CHARLES W. BRASHARES

Bishop Charles W. Brashares was elected by the 1944 North Central Jurisdiction from the pastorate of First Church, Ann Arbor, Michigan. He had succeeded Bishop Fred Fisher, who served as pastor there after resigning from the episcopacy. Bishop Brashares was the first to be elected by the North Central Jurisdiction following the establishment of the jurisdictional system. His first assignment was to the Iowa area where he served for eight years. In 1952 he moved to the Chicago area following the retirement of Bishop Magee, and he served that area until his retirement in 1964. When he went

73

to the Chicago area, it consisted of the three conferences in Illinois. In 1960 the Illinois and the Southern Illinois Conferences were removed to form a new area with Springfield as the residence. For the next four years Bishop Brashares served only the Rock River Conference.

The bishop was a short, trim man, who was partially bald. He had large eyes which had an appealing gleam. He was delightfully human, and his laughter had a boyish ring about it. He relished hearing or telling a good joke or story, always accompanying the telling with his infectious chuckle. His rare sense of humor forever stood him in good stead. No bishop was ever more genuinely friendly, cordial, or outgoing in spirit.

The bishop was always informal—in manner, in dress, in conversation, in preaching, and even in his prayers. To hear him pray was an experience. He would talk to God in a conversational way, sometimes raising questions with the Almighty, sometimes making observations, and sometime simply pouring out his heart. Those who knew him well felt that his simple childlike prayer life was one of the secrets of what he was.

Bishop Brashares had a unique way of expressing himself, and he often amused his fellow bishops by his style. One time in giving his report he began by making, with a straight face, the profound statement, "The Chicago area is named after the city of Chicago," and he got the laugh he desired. Sometimes he would take the floor to ask what seemed to be a ridiculous question or to make some outlandish proposal. The question or remark would always be accompanied by a smile, and at times the bishops did not know whether he was serious or whether he was simply testing them and having a lot of fun doing it.

The bishop was often indirect in his approach to problems and situations. He had a way of what he called "backing into things." He did not usually confront situations head-on, but with his clever wisdom and kind manner he found resolution for situations that otherwise might not have been possible.

His peculiar administrative approach which sometimes did not fall short of shrewdness served him well; in his last quadrennium he faced in a major city the strains which the turbulent sixties brought to all administrators in government, in the school world, and in the church. A number of stories shall go the rounds of the unusual way in which he handled difficult episcopal administrative responsibilities, such as the placement of some preachers who were difficult to place or the necessary retirement of ministers who were reluctant to retire.

Bishop Brashares was an informal presiding officer, casual in manner and anxious to be considerate of all. He was not a natural choice for the chair in a difficult parliamentary situation.

The bishop was a friend to all, particularly to young people. He loved them with a great love, and they in turn loved him. He had not been in the council longer than a year or two before he began to call attention to the needs of young people, and it was largely at his instigation that the Commission on Christian Vocations came into being.

Following retirement in 1964, Bishop and Mrs. Brashares moved to Evanston where they were active in First Church. After the death of Mrs. Brashares the bishop continued to make his residence at the conference home for the retired. His interest in the church and its affairs remained. He kept in his heart and prayers his episcopal colleagues long after the day when he could meet with them was past. He died in 1980.

LLOYD C. WICKE

Bishop Lloyd C. Wicke was elected by the 1948 Northeastern Jurisdictional Conference from the pastorate of Mt. Lebanon Church, Pittsburgh. He had previously been a pastor and a district superintendent in New Jersey. He was the last bishop elected who had a German Conference background. The church of his boyhood and youth was part of the Central German Conference, and he attended Baldwin Wallace, a school dear to the heart of German Methodism. His first assignment was to the Pittsburgh area which he served until 1960. The next twelve years of his active episcopacy were served in the New York area, from which he retired in 1972.

In a time when many adopted clerical garb, the bishop adhered to regular dress. A quiet, modest man, he had no use for ostentation or pretense.

Bishop Wicke has a delightful, somewhat off-hand manner. He refuses to take either himself or situations too seriously. He has a fine sense of humor and would often come up with a quick humorous remark to drive his point home. Sometimes people thought him blunt, for he is a master of the sharp retort. Though he was sometimes quick in his observations, his disposition to fairness was everywhere recognized.

Bishop Wicke was an able preacher. He was a student by nature, and this reflected itself in his messages, which were carefully written out and delivered in an easy manner. He was a craftsman in words, and his sermons had the ring of quality poetry. Usually after hearing him preach, one came away with certain unforgettable phrases of the sermon remaining in his or her mind. His marked ability in the use of words was reflected in his correspondence. He never wrote extended letters. Often a letter from him was only a single sentence, but one so vivid and complete that nothing more needed to be said.

Bishop Wicke was an active participant in the Council of Bishops and was its president in 1964. He was a good example of the participation in council affairs that makes the collective leadership of the council possible. He could be counted upon for what often proved to be "troubleshooter" responsibilities. He was regarded as something of a handyman among the bishops and capable of a variety of assignments. His perceptive mind, his openness to the opinions of others coupled with an ability to stand firm when necessary, and his tact and skill at mediation meant that the council often called upon him.

His twelve years as the resident bishop in New York included the sixties and he found himself at a focal point in the life of the nation and the church during that turbulent time. As administrator of the New York area, he had to deal with the tensions and frustrations experienced by blacks, Hispanics, and other minorities in a large metropolitan area, and he faced mounting problems of poverty, crime, and racial conflict. With calmness and firmness he sought to find creative solutions and to make genuine contributions.

The Episcopal Leadership Team 1940–1967

Some places at which Bishop Wicke took leadership under the mandate of the Council of Bishops were the establishment of what is now the Board of Church and Society (he became its first president), the creation of the Church Center at the United Nations, and the achievement of Evangelical United Brethren-Methodist union, when he served as the chairman of the Methodist contingent of the Commission on Union. He also served as chairman of the Committee on the Restructure of the Council in 1972, was a member of the committee of the council seeking to mediate the Pikeville (Kentucky) Hospital strike in 1973, and was a resource person for the Committee on the Study of the District Superintendency and the Episcopacy from 1972 to 1976. From 1968 to 1972 he was the president of the Board of Missions, the first person to serve in that capacity in the new United Methodist Church.

Bishop Wicke retired in 1972 and thereafter has made his home in Fort Myers, Florida.

JOHN WESLEY LORD

Bishop John Wesley Lord was elected by the 1948 Northeastern Jurisdictional Conference from the pastorate of First Church, Westfield, New Jersey. He was a favorite son of the Newark Conference and was only forty-six years of age at the time of his election. He was assigned to the Boston area which he served until 1960. He then served the Washington area until his retirement in 1972. Of the bishops elected in 1948 he and Bishops Wicke, Kennedy, and Short were all to see twenty-four years of active service, a record probably not to be equaled in the future due to the General Conference's twice lowering the mandatory retirement age.

Full of energy, Bishop Lord has an engaging smile and a contagious warmth of spirit. He could do a job upon social occasions that few could match, and it was said that his handling of the Committee on Courtesies in the Jurisdictional Conference at which he was elected created many admirers for him. He is always cordial and outgoing.

The bishop is a decided liberal, particularly in his thinking on social questions. Like several of his episcopal colleagues, he was a disciple of Bishop Oxnam, and in turn Bishop Oxnam was attached to him. In the council, Bishop Lord unhesitatingly spoke his convictions and accorded those who differed with him the same privilege. He readily took public stands on controversial issues or signed manifestos which he felt merited his signature. In the days of the freedom marches in the South he put in his appearance. He did not speak too often in the Council of Bishops, but when he did, some social issue was probably under consideration. He would usually write out his thoughts and then speak from his notes. The council honored him by making him its president in 1970.

One of Bishop Lord's interests is the racial situation. He is by nature the friend of the downtrodden and the oppressed, particularly those who suffer because of color. He favored eliminating from the polity of the church structures based upon race. In cooperation with Bishop Edgar Love of the Central Jurisdiction whose Baltimore area overlapped the Washington area, he pioneered in breaking segregation patterns prior to 1964 when the racial conferences within the Northeasterm Jurisdiction became a part of the jurisdiction and were absorbed in the geographic conferences. He was one of the first bishops to make local church appointments across racial lines.

Bishop Lord retired in 1972. The church soon called him out of retirement to promote the Bishops' Program for Peace and the Self-Development of Peoples. This was a natural assignment for someone with his strong social conscience. He gave about two years to this assignment and then resigned; Bishop Ralph Dodge succeeded him.

In retirement Bishop and Mrs. Lord have chosen to live in New Hampshire during the summer months and in Lakeland, Florida, in the winter.

ROY H. SHORT

Bishop Roy H. Short was elected by the 1948 Southeastern Jurisdictional Conference. He was at the time editor of The *Upper Room*. Previously he had served pastorates and districts in the Louisville Conference, his last pastorate being St. Paul's, Louisville. He was assigned to the newly created Jacksonville area consisting of the Florida and Cuba

Conferences and was the first resident bishop of Florida Methodism. After four years on the Jacksonville area, he served the Nashville area for twelve years and the Louisville area for eight, retiring in 1972. From 1956 to 1972 he was the secretary of the Council of Bishops. Following retirement, he and Mrs. Short have made their home in Nashville, Tennessee.

Attempt at a self-portrait involves necessarily seeing one's self from within as well as from without, as others see one. And to see one's self from within is inevitably to be made aware of limitations. Upon coming into the council, Bishop Short found himself amazed at the strength and insight of many of its members, and he suffered from a considerable amount of self-consciousness upon the realization that he was now a member of such an august body. For eight years, therefore, he played largely an observer's role, hesitating to participate in debate, being unsure of the ability to make any particular contribution, and seldom being called upon for an assignment. In 1956 the council found itself almost hopelessly at a loss when its gifted, efficient, and assertive secretary for sixteen years, Bishop Oxnam, was forced by health reasons to ask that he not be reelected. Bishop Short was elected secretary largely because Bishop Titus Lowe and Bishop Arthur J. Moore passed the word that he had been for seventeen years a conference secretary.

The secretaryship of the council necessarily involved for Bishop Short a larger degree of participation in council affairs than had been his during his first eight years of membership. He continued as secretary for sixteen years until reaching the age of retirement.

RICHARD C. RAINES

Bishop Richard C. Raines was elected by the 1948 North Central Jurisdictional Conference from the pastorate of Hennepin Avenue Church in Minneapolis. He was the first of four bishops elected by that jurisdictional conference. A groundswell had developed in his direction, and it was generally expected that he would be elected soon after the conference began balloting. For some time he had been one of the "fair-haired boys" of the church in that day, frequently called upon for platform appearances far and wide. He was assigned to the Indiana area, which he served the entire time of his active episcopacy, a total of twenty years.

Bishop Raines was tall, trim, and athletic. He loved swimming and other sports and continued his participation in them well into the days of his retirement. He was affable and good-natured and enjoyed being in good company. He entered readily into conversation but never monopolized it. He drew out of the opinion of others and left them impressed with how pleasant the conservation had been.

He was broad in his thinking and did not hesitate to express his opinion and to take a stand. This he would do with grace, keeping his emotions under control. He was quite understanding of those who differed from him.

Bishop Raines was a popular preacher. Prior to his election he held strong pulpits, and as a bishop he continued to major in preaching. He was called upon for preaching engagements throughout the church. His sermons were usually addressed to life situations and to issues of current concern. He would take a passage from the Bible and relate it to the questions and problems of his audience. It was a disappointment to many who admired Bishop Raines's pulpit ability that he did almost no writing for publication.

The bishop was a careful and considerate administrator, who worked well with his cabinets and pastors. He took a special interest in young preachers, and he tried to spot those of promise and give them their chance even as an earlier bishop had given him his chance. He did not hesitate to go across the country to find promising young preachers and bring them to Indiana.

Bishop Raines was highly respected in the Council of Bishops and was often given special assignments. He served as its president in 1966.

A world traveler, the bishop was much interested in the overseas work of the church. He was for a quadrennium president of the Board of Missions. During his last quadrennium as an active bishop, he was the chairman of the Commission on the Structure of Methodism Overseas. He took great interest in this assignment and devoted endless hours to it. He joined those who felt that the time had come for the churches overseas to become autonomous if that was their choice, but the churches were not of one mind on that issue. The quadrennium during which Bishop Raines served as chairman witnessed the beginning of the dismantling of what had long been a world church when the churches in Latin America and Southeast Asia chose autonomy. In 1980 India was to make the same choice.

Upon his retirement Bishop Raines was given a special assignment by the Council of Bishops in the field of enlistment. He gave himself to this with enthusiasm and found a fine response. Young people admired him, and many of them responded to his urging to yield to the call of God, as it came to them, and find a place in the ministry or in church-related vocations.

After retirement, Bishop and Mrs. Raines made their home in Pompano Beach, Florida, in the winter, and Glen Arbor, Michigan, in the summer. In 1979 they changed their winter home to Lakeland, Florida.

Bishop Raines died suddenly in 1981, Mrs. Raines having preceded him in death by only a few months.

HAZEN G. WERNER

Bishop Hazen C. Werner was elected by the 1948 North Central Jurisdictional Conference. At the time he was on the faculty of Drew Seminary, but previous to that he had been pastor of churches in Michigan and Ohio. He was assigned to the Ohio area, which at that time embraced all the territory included now in two episcopal areas—the Ohio East and the Ohio West. He served this area until 1964 when he took over the supervision of the work in Hong Kong and Taiwan. There he served until his retirement in 1968.

Though pleasant, Bishop Werner was generally all-business and absorbed in whatever he was doing. His personal resources and self-reliance helped him to be firm if occasion demanded.

The bishop was a popular preacher. There was a humanness about his preaching, which was quiet and almost casual in manner, replete with human interest stories and wise observations. He knew well how to hold the attention of his audience, and he was in demand for platform appearances everywhere.

Bishop Werner attended the council meetings regularly but was one of its less active participants. He sat quietly and thoughtfully in his place, entering only occasionally into the discussions. While he was an active bishop twenty years, he never held office in the council. This did not seem to matter to him.

The bishop was interested in many fields, particularly in the field of family life. It was here that he won his spurs. He was a pioneer in developing in Methodism a concern for the problems of the family. This in part spotted him for consideration for the episcopacy. He worked with the Board of Evangelism as it sought to contribute in this field, and he was the chairman of its Committee on Family Life. He was the leader of the first family life conference sponsored by the Board of Evangelism at Clear Lake, Iowa, in 1947. After his election to the episcopacy, he became chairman of the Family Life Committee of the entire church and was for years the leading figure in the Quadrennial Family Life Conference. In due time he sold the Methodist World Council upon the idea of a World Family Life Movement, and he led in this for a long period. The bishop also did much writing on family life; a number of his books enjoyed a wide circulation.

Bishop Werner was a traveler by nature, and his travels carried him to all parts of the world. He recognized that the problems of the family in which he was so much interested were problems in every land as well as his own, and he therefore sought to give impetus to a world family life movement.

For some years the Council of Bishops gave him a liaison assignment with the autonomous church of Korea. He took great interest in this assignment and discharged it with dispatch. Since his interests were worldwide, it is not surprising that the council asked him to give his last active years in the episcopacy to the Hong Kong-Taiwan area, where he wrote a record of helpfulness.

Upon retirement Bishop Werner moved to his farm in Vermont. Mrs. Werner was seriously ill, and her illness lengthened into years. The bishop gave her his full attention and set a beautiful example of the family devotion he had preached for so long.

Followed the passing of Mrs. Werner, the bishop moved to Lake Wales, Florida, and later to St Petersburg. In his later years he has only rarely attended the meetings of the council.

GERALD KENNEDY

Bishop Gerald Kennedy was elected by the Western Jurisdiction in 1948. At the time he was not a member of that jurisdiction but was pastor of St. Paul Church, Lincoln, Nebraska, in the South Central Jurisdiction. He had received some votes for bishop in the South Central Jurisdictional Conference which met a few days earlier. His was one of the two elections across jurisdictional lines; the other was that of Bishop Lorenzo King in 1944. The story has it that Bishop Kennedy was playing baseball at the time he was notified of his election.

His first assignment was to the Portland area which had been left vacant by the death of Bishop Bruce Baxter. After four years, he was assigned to the Los Angeles area upon the retirement of Bishop Baker, and he served there until his retirement in 1972.

Bishop Kennedy was a short, wiry, athletic man who loved baseball, swimming, and other sports. He could easily have been mistaken for a farmer bronzed by the sun. He went hatless long before that practice was common, and he was informal in his dress and casual in his manner. In the day when he began his episcopacy, he would not have been identified readily with the popular image of bishops as impressive in size or height, dignified in bearing, reserved, decidedly clerical, and sometimes even pompous.

Bishop Kennedy's marvelous sense of humor enhanced his abilities as a master storyteller. He abhorred what he called a "stuffed shirt," and he had a particular power to detect sham and pretense, which he heartily despised. His quick mind often made it difficult for him to be patient with persons who labored a question or were slow to make decisions. He sometimes seemed somewhat offhand in his manner of approaching a problem or in presiding in a meeting, and persons who did not know him well sometimes took this for indifference.

Bishop Kennedy did not enjoy the administrative side of the episcopacy. Matters that were largely routine seemed to bore him. When he could delegate such responsibilities, he gladly did.

An omnivorous reader the bishop probably read more extensively than any member of the council in his day. He would rise early and soon bury himself in a book. He read as he traveled, and he has told this writer of times when reading in an airport, he became so absorbed that he let the plane depart without him. His love of reading resulted in his writing book reviews for national magazines.

Bishop Kennedy belonged to the liberal school of thought and was committed to social action. Living daily with the problems of the church and its mission to people, he began to sense increasingly the need for a stronger emphasis upon evangelism. This conviction sounded in his preaching and lectures and appeared in his writings. However, he entertained no shallow conception of evangelism; he thought of it as seeking the redemption of all of life, redemption of both persons and the society in which their lives had to be lived. For some years he was chairman of the former Board of Evangelism, and he gave it significant leadership.

Bishop Kennedy was primarily a preacher who loved to preach, and the pulpit was his throne. So effective was his preaching that he will long hold a place in the minds of not only United Methodists but also of others as one of the truly great American preachers of recent years. He was a scriptural preacher who made the Book come alive for his hearers. His keen observations challenged his audience, and he held their attention by using illustrations and human interest material. His messages were practical. He refused to dodge social issues and dealt with them realistically and forthrightly. Always he demanded that the thought behind his sermons be applied to life.

He believed there was no substitute for effective preaching, and he constantly urged the members of his conference to feed the flock of Christ. His sermons at his Annual Conferences were for preachers and lay delegates the highlight of rich days together. He was one of the few Methodist bishops to deliver the Lyman Beecher Lectures at Yale, the only other of later years being Bishop Oxnam. Toward the end of his episcopacy Bishop Kennedy returned to his first love—taking over the pulpit of First Church, Pasadena. There he continued to preach to large congregations until serious illness forced him to lay aside his loved employ.

Bishop Kennedy was an active participant in the Council of Bishops. There was a back row in his day, as there has usually been a back row in the council. Then it included Bishops Corson, Angie Smith, and Ensley in addition to Bishop Kennedy. The occupants of the back row did not sit quietly and watch the rest of the group operate. Each of them would sally forth when felt led to do so. Occasionally Bishop Kennedy would take the floor to make a pertinent, brief remark, to move that some particular action be taken, or even to suggest that the discussion was getting nowhere and that we might as well adjourn.

Although Bishop Kennedy sometimes seemed bored with the meetings of the council, no bishop actually relished them more. He wrote in his book *The Parables of Jesus:* "I am never more aware of the exuberance and joy of life than when I am in a meeting of the Council of Bishops." He was president of the council from 1960-1961.

Many honors came to Bishop Kennedy, but he took them in stride and was never puffed up. When he retired as president of the National Division of the Board of Missions, a banquet was arranged in his honor, but he could not get there. He wrote those in charge, "Hang a wreath on my chair."

DONALD HARVEY TIPPETT

Bishop Tippett was elected in the 1948 Western Jurisdictional Conference from the pastorate of First Church, Los Angeles. Of the three elected by that Jurisdictional Conference, two bishops—Glenn Phillips and Donald Tippett—were both members of the Southern California Conference and pastors in adjoining communities. Bishop Tippett had earlier held other distinguished pulpits, including Bexley Church, Columbus, Ohio, and the Church of All Nations in New York. He was assigned to the San Francisco area, which he served until his retirement in 1968.

The bishop was tall, straight shouldered and quick in his movements. One of his eyes looked in a different direction from the other, as a result of an injury inflicted when a street gang attacked him when he was pastor of the Church of All Nations. He took the attack philosophically, bore no grudge toward those who had injured him, and even made a joke of his impairment. He used to boast that he was the only bishop who could occupy the chair and see all the delegates when they were seated horizontally to the chair in a great auditorium. His unfailing sense of humor and jovial, friendly manner made him good company.

The bishop had an unusually strong voice, which he did not choose to modulate. He could be heard above everybody else in conversation. He talked on the telephone in the same strong voice, and his brother bishops used to ask him whether he thought that in making a long distance call he actually had to make himself heard across the miles involved.

Physically, Bishop Tippett seemed indestructible. He traveled incessantly and never seemed to weary. On several occasions he was so seriously ill that friends thought they would never see him again, but he would bounce back and soon be his active self. On one occasion during the sixties when the council was due to meet in his area, the Executive Committee considered moving the place of meeting to another Western Jurisdiction city because they feared he would not be alive when the date came. The decision was not made, however, and when the meeting was held, he was his usual self.

Bishop Tippett was not afflicted with modesty, and he was anything but timid and retiring. While he gave the impression of thinking well of himself, he was at the same time brotherly in his expression of appreciation of others.

The bishop had been a pulpit figure prior to his election, and afterward he continued in that role. He was constantly in

The Episcopal Leadership Team 1940–1967

demand for pulpit and platform appearances not only throughout the United States but also over much of the world. He was also a scholarly lecturer, and many colleges and universities invited him to speak. His lectures covered a wide range, and a number of them found their way into print and enjoyed general distribution.

Bishop Tippett led the Methodist Church into a wider use of films, radio, and television. At the time he entered the episcopal ranks some Methodist preachers over the country were experimenting with local radio programs of various kinds, and at least one Methodist preacher, Dr. Ralph Sockman, had acquired a national reputation through a nationwide broadcast which lasted for thirty-six years, the National Radio Pulpit.

Some agencies of the church were doing limited work in radio and films, such as the Board of Missions under Dr. Harry Spencer, the Board of Education under Dr. Howard Tower, and the Board of Evangelism under Dr. Harry Williams, but the church as a whole had no unified program in this field. The 1948 General Conference took notice of this need and instructed the Council of Secretaries, the Women's Society of Christian Service, and the Publishing House to move into the field, but it provided no funds.

The various agencies named representatives to a joint committee, and the Council of Bishops named Bishop Tippett as a member. He served as chairman and gave vigorous and creative leadership for four years. The final result was the creation by the 1952 General Conference of the Radio and Film Commission. Bishop Tippett became president, and Dr. Harry Spencer became the executive secrtary. The two men made an ideal team, for Dr. Spencer had the expertise and Bishop Tippett had the forcefulness, the drive, and the refusal to be overwhelmed that were necessary in their positions.

Bishop Tippett was greatly interested in theological education. In his day a bishop was allowed to be an officer of more than one agency, and in addition to being an officer of TRAFCO (Television, Radio, and Film Commission), he was the chairman of the Department of the Ministry of the Board of Education. In this position, too, he gave significant leadership. He championed the idea that the theological schools were a churchwide responsibility. In the 1956 General Conference he was a chief sponsor of the action that resulted in the establishment of Ohio Seminary at Delaware, Ohio, and of St. Paul at Kansas City. He was followed in this office by Bishop Everett W. Palmer, who took leadership, supported by the veteran educator Bishop Fred G. Holloway, in the establishment of the Fund for Ministerial Education, which has become a permanent and most important feature of the financial structure of The United Methodist Church.

Bishop Tippett was an ardent student. His bedroom was also his study, and it was piled high with books stacked on top of each other, magazines, newspapers, and an amazing clutter of all kinds of material. When he had thus filled a room, Mrs. Tippett would give him another one, and he would repeat the process. When the writer visited him in his home in 1968, he was on his third room. The amazing thing was that he somehow knew how to find whatever it was he wanted.

The bishop was a liberal in his theology and was a social activist. From his early years as the pastor of the Church of All Nations to the end of his days, he kept the dream of seeing the kingdom of God come upon earth.

Bishop Tippett was a careful administrator who gave close attention to his area. He was an active participant in the activities of the Council of Bishops and was its president at the time of union with the Evangelical United Brethren Church in 1968.

Bishop Tippett retired in 1968 and continued to make his home in Berkeley, California. He preached practically every Sunday throughout the first ten years of his retirement and continued lecturing in colleges and universities. After retirement he ceased to attend the meetings of the council or the General Conference. He did, at the invitation of Bishop Marvin Stuart, attend the meeting of the council at Colorado Springs in 1978, and he spoke at the episcopal family dinner. He had changed greatly in his appearance since the episcopal family had seen him last. With his long white hair, some said he reminded them of some pictures of Father Wesley. Many of the bishops with whom he had companied, had either gone on

THE EPISCOPAL LEADERSHIP TEAM 1940–1967

or were themselves no longer able to travel, and with so many new bishops whom he had not known he found himself a stranger in a strange company and tarried only for the night, returning to his home early in the next morning.

Bishop Tippett died in March, 1982.

JOSE VALENCIA

Bishop Jose Valencia was elected by the 1948 Philippines Central Conference. He had for some years been a pastor and district superintendent. He had won great respect for the valiant way he had carried on his duties during the time of the Japanese occupation. He was the second Filipino to be elected to the episcopal office. For almost twenty years he supervised the entire Philippine work. The General Conference finally recognized that this was too heavy an assignment for one bishop and authorized the election of a second one. The work was then divided into the Manila and Baguio areas, and Bishop Valencia administered the Baguio area until his retirement in 1968.

Bishop Valencia's vitality and stamina enabled him to endure the wear of continually traveling his far-flung ecclesiastical island empire. The bishop quietly carried on his administration and faced tense situations in a calm way. This same quietness marked his chairmanship of a conference. The Philippine Methodists exceed all Methodists in the world in their enthusiasm for church law and their habit of raising legal questions, and they sometimes do not make it too easy for the presiding officer. When in the chair, Bishop Valencia would keep his poise, reflect for a moment upon the point raised, and then give his answer in a measured voice.

Bishop Valencia was devoted in his administration. Every project in his area received his attention, and in his frequent visits to the United States he was constantly making new friends for the work in the Philippines. He attended the meetings of the Council of Bishops on an average of once a year. There he usually sat thoughtfully, entering into the discussions only when it seemed to him that the matter under discussion had pertinence to the work in his area.

Bishop Valencia is above all an evangelist. His great

concern is to reach people for Christ, and at this he has been eminently successful. He becomes greatly disturbed whenever he detects in the church any lessening of evangelistic passion. He makes much of prayer. For a brother bishop to room with him was a humbling experience, for the roommate soon discovered how much time Bishop Valencia spent on his knees.

Following his retirement, Bishop Valencia has written the story of his life, continues to preach often, and maintains his interest in every phase of the life of the church not only in the Philippines but also in the rest of the world.

SANTE U. BARBIERI

Bishop Sante U. Barbieri was elected by the 1949 Latin American Central Conference, from the directorship of the seminary in Buenos Aires. He was born in Italy, grew up in Brazil, and spent his early ministry in both Brazil and Argentina. He was assigned to the Buenos Aires area which included the work in Argentina, Uruguay, and Bolivia. He continued to serve this area until his retirement in 1968.

Bishop Barbieri is a linguist who speaks four languages with ease. He is a genuine scholar, with special interest in theology and social ethics. He reads constantly and is fully familiar with various schools of thought. His deep personal convictions appear in his sermons and in his gifted writing. He has written often for the press and published a number of books.

Bishop Barbieri is a poet. His rare facility with words, enables him to create beauty of both idea and expression. He can convert long hours of plane travel into an opportunity to express his thoughts in a new poem. Sometimes in the bishops' meetings he would sit quietly, apparently lost in thought, and the outcome would be some choice gem of fresh poetry.

The bishop is a good preacher, who relies heavily up on the Bible in his preaching. He selects an idea he wants to convey and then finds a biblical passage ideally fitted to it. His ability to do this is almost uncanny.

Bishop Barbieri was a good administrator. He was creative in his planning of the work of his area, and he knew how to find and develop leadership for the church. Some of the young ministers whom he discovered and encouraged have become strong leaders in both Methodism and the ecumenical church. When the bishop occupied the chair, he was a deliberate, steady presiding officer.

The bishop is a staunch ecumenist and is recognized for his ecumenical activity. Particularly in his own Latin America has he taken leadership in ecumenical affairs. From 1954 to 1961 he was one of the presidents of the World Council of Churches. He was also a vice-president of the World Council on Christian Education for a period. With so many responsibilities as both a bishop and an ecumenical leader he traveled almost constantly, but he did not seem to weary and was never heard to complain.

The Methodist Church in Latin America had some great episcopal leaders in the course of its long history, but three made especially indelible impressions. The first was Bishop William F. Oldham. The second was Bishop George Miller. And the third was Bishop Barbieri. For twenty years he was a leading figure in the life of Methodism in Latin America, and little happened without his blessing. He was committed to the autonomous church pattern, and during the Cosmos discussions (1964 to 1968) he advocated this position. Largely due to his leadership, in 1968 Methodism in Argentina, Chile, Peru, Bolivia, and Uruguay became independent national churches electing their leaders, while Panama and Costa Rica entered into church unions.

Bishop Barbieri retired in 1968. Though the churches with which he had long been associated were now independent churches, only related to The United Methodist Church, he continued a member of the Council of Bishops under the Disciplinary provision that Central Conference bishops reaching retirement age while in office continue as council members.

After he retired, Bishop Barbieri made his home in Buenos Aires. He continues to preach, lecture, and write and to take leadership in a newly formed association of Latin American Methodist churches created to continue in some measure the association represented by the former Central Conference.

FREDERICK B. NEWELL

Bishop Frederick B. Newell was elected by the 1952 Northeastern Jurisdictional Conference. At the time he had been for some years the executive of the New York City Society. He was a son of New York, and New York was not only in his blood but also in his heart. In his early ministry he was associated with Frank Mason North, and with him he shared the dream that the cities of earth might each become the city of God. He was the friend of the poor, the exploited, and the victims of social wrong. He was particularly concerned about the plight of immigrants and ethnic minorities. He was creative in his leadership, and Methodism in New York will long be marked by the indelible stamp of his influence. Upon his election he was assigned to the New York area, which he served until retirement in 1960. Following the sudden death of Bishop Middleton, he was recalled from retirement to serve the Pittsburgh area for two years.

Bishop Newell kept in good physical trim, and was a devotee of golf, playing regularly even into his eighties. He came of a business family and was himself an excellent businessman. None of the bishops of his day knew more about the market and investments than did he, though he emphasized the idea that what one has is always relative, and whether one is rich or poor depends upon the person with whom one is compared. The bishop lived well but was never ostentatious.

Bishop Newell was a Chesterfield among the bishops. He was faultless in manner and a devotee of the fine amenities of life. On every occasion he knew exactly what was proper, and he conducted himself accordingly. In debate he spoke deliberately and thoughtfully.

For many years prior to his election Bishop Newell was a familiar floor figure in each General Conference. He was one of those delegates who helped to keep a General Conference moving. He knew how to cut through a tangled and lengthening debate and make a motion that would bring matters to a head. He was given many assignments during his days as a delegate, and he efficiently discharged all of them. Strangely enough, after he had been a General Conference floor leader for so long, as a bishop he never presided in a General Conference. This was, however, according to his wish.

The Episcopal Leadership Team 1940–1967

Following his second retirement in 1968, Bishop Newell spent the winter months in the South, and the balance of the year in his Connecticut home not far from his beloved New York. He died in 1979. Although he was the oldest of the bishops elected in 1952, he outlived all of them; Bishops Coors, Watts, Grant, and Branscomb died while still active and Bishops Voight, Ensley, Clair, and Love after retirement.

FRIEDRICH WUNDERLICH

Bishop Friedrich Wunderlich was elected by the Germany Central Conference in 1953 from the presidency of the seminary at Frankfurt. Early in his ministry he had served as a pastor or on special assignment, but the fifteen years prior to his election had been given to the seminary either as professor or president. His father was a minister, and he came of a family identified with Methodism from its beginning days in Germany.

The bishop is a thorough scholar. He has authored numerous books and articles. Although he always enjoyed the quiet hours of scholarly study, he chose to be much involved in the stressful world about him. He is an observant person, and his comments in council meetings concerning current issues were incisive and pertinent. One of his major concerns has been world peace which is only logical since he has known personally the agony of war.

At the time of Bishop Wunderlich's administration, he was able to travel freely and to supervise the entire work in Germany, which he did with admirable efficiency. He thus served not only as an administering bishop but also as a personal link shuttling back and forth between the Methodists of a divided land. In 1970 the time came at last when certain restrictions arose which made it necessary to establish a Central Conference in East Germany. Bishop Armin Härtel was elected its first bishop.

At the time of Bishop Wunderlich's election the Methodist Church in Germany, to a large degree, still needed to recover from the devastation of the war. The bishop gave strong leadership to a program of reconstruction and rehabilitation at which he was highly successful. He traveled extensively in the United States, where he found welcome response to his story of the needs of the German church.

The church called upon Bishop Wunderlich in both his active days and his retirement for his services beyond his native Germany. While he was still active, he visited the church in Cuba when the American bishop who held the assignment could not get into the country. After he had retired in 1964, upon the death of Bishop Hagen he took over the work in Scandinavia until a new bishop could be elected. For a period he cared for the Geneva office of the World Methodist Council. In retirement the bishop continues to make his home in Frankfurt.

HOBART B. AMSTUTZ

Bishop Hobart B. Amstutz was elected by the 1956 Central Conference of Southeast Asia. He had been a missionary in Malaysia for many years and had held various posts as pastor, district superintendent, and professor, and school head. There had been strong sentiment in the Central Conference for some time for the election of a national, but the conference represented so many diverse national and ethnic groups that agreement could not be reached upon what national representative to elect. The conference settled the matter by turning to the election of an appreciated missionary—in 1950 Bishop Archer, in 1956 Bishop Amstutz, and in 1964 Bishop Lundy. In 1968 it elected Bishop Yap Kim How, a Chinese pastor.

Following his election Bishop Amstutz supervised a vast area including the work in Singapore, Malaysia, Indonesia, Sarawak, and Burma. It was while he was bishop that both Burma and Indonesia became independent churches. He continued to supervise the work in Singapore, Malaysia, and Sarawak until his retirement in 1964. He was then called upon by the Council of Bishops to take charge of the work in Pakistan after Bishop Rockey had to ask to be relieved of this responsibility. Bishop Amstutz cared for the work in Pakistan until the church there became independent.

Bishop Amstutz regarded the episcopacy as a high honor and conducted himself accordingly with great dignity. He liked ecclesiastical habiliments and enjoyed religious ceremony. He delighted in formal occasions, and found that many Methodists of this area responded heartily to them.

The bishop was a careful administrator who paid great attention to details. His reports on his work were always comprehensive and calculated to enlist support. With his area covering so vast an expanse, he had to be on the road much of the time. In covering his territory he traveled by plane, train, car, and jeep, even by longboat up river in Sarawak. As he carried on his work he would find himself at one time in the fine home of some Methodist in Singapore or Penang and again in a longhouse of the Ibans set in the midst of the jungle. Certainly no bishop of the church administered an area marked by more variety. In Malaya alone there were Chinese, Malaysians, Tamils, and persons of British, American, or European background, to say nothing of the differences found throughout the remainder of the episcopal area.

Bishop Amstutz attended the meetings of the Council of Bishops with fair regularity. He greatly enjoyed them, although he did not usually take the floor except when something was under discussion related to the work of the church overseas from the United States.

Bishop Amstutz had an experience that brought him great distress in the late days of his life. He had assumed that when he reached retirement age he would continue as a bishop of the church. The council assumed the same thing, for it called upon him as a retired bishop to care for the work in Pakistan. In 1966 a question was raised in the Philippines regarding the status of Bishop Alejandro who had been elected a term bishop and who had served to retirement age. The matter went to the Judicial Council, which ruled that a term bishop who reached retirement age was no longer a bishop but was a former bishop. This decision affected not only Bishop Alejandro, but also Bishops Balloch, Archer, and Amstutz. Bishop Alejandro was greatly disappointed in the decision, but he accepted it philosophically, though regretfully. Bishop Archer and Bishop Balloch made no protest.

Bishop Amstutz, however, could not bring himself to losing membership in the Council of Bishops without a battle. He began an endeavor to recover his membership. He wrote letters, entered pleas, and made contacts which he hoped would help. Though he was technically no longer a bishop, the council left him in charge in Pakistan and sent a bishop at conference time to care for the ordinations. Some of the bishops interceded personally for Bishop Amstutz, trying to find some way to effect his restoration. Some friends also introduced legislation in the 1968 General Conference that might effect his and the other bishops' restoration, but the Judicial Council declared such legislation could not be retroactive. Bishop Amstutz did not surrender, however, and neither did his friends.

At last in the 1976 General Conference, legislation was passed which took care of the matter. Bishop Amstutz and Bishop Balloch were returned to the roll of the council. By that time Bishop Alejandro and Bishop Archer were deceased.

Though feeble and frail, Bishop Amstutz began to attend once more the meetings of the council, with the relish with which he had attended them in his days as an active bishop. He died in 1980.

RALPH E. DODGE

Bishop Ralph E. Dodge was elected by the 1956 Africa Central Conference. He was at the time the African secretary of the Board of Missions. For some years previous to that he had been a greatly loved missionary in Angola. He was one of four missionaries to Africa elected to the episcopacy. The others were Bishops Springer, Booth, and Andreassen. Bishop Booth had carried the Africa assignment alone for twelve years, and with the election of Bishop Dodge the work was divided among them. Bishop Dodge was assigned to care for Rhodesia, Angola, and Mozambique.

Bishop Dodge was committed to the election of national leadership, and it brought great joy to his heart when the first native Africans, Bishops Shungu and Zunguze, were elected in 1964. Upon the retirement of Bishop Dodge in 1968, Bishop Abel Muzorewa, another native African, was elected. Bishops de Carvalho and Fama Onema were elected in 1972, which was the first time the College of Bishops of the African Central Conference was composed entirely of native leadership. The dream of Bishop Dodge for many years had come true at last.

Bishop Dodge has profound convictions, which he never hesitated to express on the platform, in debate, or in writing. He passionately believes that all people, regardless of race, previous condition, social status, or educational level, are God's children and are entitled to the same freedoms, advantages, and proper recognition. He is a bitter foe of all exploitation or other mistreatment of individuals. He is forever on the side of the oppressed and the disadvantaged not only in the Africa he loves so dearly but also anywhere else in the world. He speaks out when he feels the need, and his outspokenness sometimes invites reaction. In 1964 he was exiled from Rhodesia by the white government and was forced to administer his area from a base in neighboring Zambia.

About midcentury Bishop Dodge came to realize that the era of the traditional missionary was almost over. Though the bishop had been a missionary himself, he accepted this. He rejoiced that the harvest time of the gospel had come and that the long years of consecrated missionary endeavor had now produced native sons and daughters ably qualified to undertake full responsibility. This conviction made him do all he could to encourage national leadership at strategic points in the life of the church. It was natural that in the Council of Bishops he should plead so often for the fullest involvement of the Central Conference bishops.

Bishop Dodge retired in 1968 at the age of sixty-two. He was in good health, and with his peculiar gifts the council called upon him for a variety of services. When Bishop Sigg died in 1965, the council put Bishop Dodge in charge of a part of the Geneva area until a new bishop could be elected. When Bishop Muzorewa became prime minister of Zimbabwe and asked to be relieved of episcopal responsibilities for a period, the council called upon Bishop Dodge to take over. When a political situation developed in Liberia in 1980 that made it impossible for Bishop Warner, who had been in the United States for General Conference, to return, the council asked Bishop Dodge to hold the Central Conference and preside over the election of a new bishop. During the 1976 to 1980 quadrennium the council asked Bishop Dodge to take over the promotion of the Peace Emphasis, after Bishop Lord asked to be released.

Upon retirement Bishop Dodge became chaplain of Mindola Ecumenical Institute in Zambia where he served for some time. Later he and Mrs. Dodge made their home in Springfield, Missouri, for some years and then moved to Dowling Park, Florida. Mrs. Dodge died in 1982.

EUGENE M. FRANK

Bishop Eugene M. Frank was elected by the 1956 South Central Jurisdictional Conference from the pastorate of First Church, Topeka, Kansas. Previous to that he had served several other pastorates in Kansas. He was the first bishop elected by the South Central Jurisdiction from its Kansas and Nebraska section and the first having a Methodist Episcopal background. At the time of union in 1939 one of the difficult questions to be faced was where to allocate the work in Kansas and Nebraska. The work there had all been Methodist Episcopal, and it would have been quite natural to have aligned it with the North Central Jurisdiction. However in an attempt to balance the jurisdictions in strength, the decision finally was to place the conferences of these two states in the South Central Jursidiction. Historians give Bishop Ainsworth credit for this suggestion, and the Joint Commission accepted it. All the other states in the South Central Jurisdiction respresented predominantly the work of the Methodist Episcopal Church, South. At first the conferences in Kansas and Nebraska did not feel themselves too intimately a part of the jurisdiction.

Attempts were made in 1944, 1948, and 1952 to elect a bishop with a Kansas or Nebraska background, but all of them failed. The election of Bishop Frank in 1956 meant that section of the jurisdiction was represented in the College of Bishops for the first time. No other bishops were elected from the Kansas-Nebraska section until the election of Bishop Holter in 1972.

Bishop Frank was assigned to the St. Louis area to follow Bishop Ivan Lee Holt. Unlike Bishop Holt, who was a world traveler and frequently absent from his area, Bishop Frank chose to give the area a close pastoral administration. He served the St. Louis area for sixteen years, after which he served the Arkansas area until his retirement in 1976. He found the Arkansas area a great joy to serve, since it was largely rural in character and had few of the problems of urbanization represented by the St. Louis area.

The bishop is a high-minded man. Unworthy methods to achieve a desired end or cheap politics have always met with the abhorrence of his soul.

Bishop Frank has a talent for music. He is a good singer, and he sings the songs of Zion with spirit and understanding.

The bishop was a faithful member of the council, always in his place. He did not take the floor too often, although his reactions and quiet asides, spoken to those who sat near him, were always of interest. He served as president of the council from 1968 to 1969, during which time he tried to improve the council's working procedures.

Bishop Frank retired in 1976. With his longtime emphasis upon the pastoral role, it is not surprising that Candler School of Theology called him to share his rich pastoral experiences for four years with its student body.

In 1980 Bishop Frank resumed his beloved pastoral role as he joined the staff of Central Church, Kansas City, as bishop in residence.

NOLAN B. HARMON

Bishop Nolan B. Harmon was elected by the 1956 Southeastern Jurisdictional Conference. At the time of his election he was book editor of the church. Prior to that he had been pastor of Green Memorial, Roanoke, Virginia. He was a leader in the old Baltimore Conference of the M. E. Church, South, which at the time of union was merged into the Virginia and Baltimore Conferences of the new church. Its ministry and membership were thus divided not only between two Annual Conferences but also between two jurisdictions. At the division Bishop Harmon fell into the Virginia Conference.

His episcopal assignment was to the Charlotte area, which he served until his retirement in 1964. When he went to

Charlotte, the area included the Western North Carolina and the South Carolina Conferences. In 1960 the South Carolina Conference was constituted a separate area. Bishop Hodge died in 1961, and Bishop Harmon then took over the North Alabama Conference for the remainder of the quadrennium. For one year during the illness of Bishop Watkins, he also assumed responsibility for the Kentucky Conference.

The bishop is a son of the Old South. His Mississippi, Maryland, and Virginia background is reflected in much that he has thought and said and done. He is ever the dignified, courteous Southern gentleman. He has a formality that came out even in his manner of presiding in the General Conference.

Bishop Harmon belongs to the category of the scholar in the episcopacy. Books began to come from his hand as a young preacher, several of which remained standards for more than one generation of preachers. As book editor he made quite a name for himself; perhaps his greatest contribution in that role was the publication of *The Interpreter's Bible*. In retirement he edited the *Encyclopedia of World Methodism*, for which the church will be in debt to him for generations to come.

Much of his work has been done in the field of church polity and church law. His counsel on legal matters was often sought in the council. He tended in legal interpretations to take viewpoints which were traditional in the M. E. Church, South. His interest in hymnody, particularly the texts of hymns, helped him to make a large contribution as a member of the Commission on the Hymnal.

Bishop Harmon participated fully in the discussions of the Council of Bishops, especially when legal points were under consideration. He was never an officer of the council, due undoubtedly to the shortness of the number of years that he was an active bishop. The devotional messages which he brought to this council upon occasion made a deep impression upon his fellow bishops for their scholarliness, wisdom, and pertinence.

Following his retirement he moved to Atlanta and began to teach classes in Candler School of Theology. He was popular with the students, and they flocked to his classes. He was still going strong in his teaching when he had reached the age of ninety.

MANGAL SINGH

Bishop Mangal Singh was elected by the Southern Asia Central Conference in 1956. He had served as a pastor and a district superintendent and in church promotional work in the North India Conference and the Delhi Annual Conference. He was a member of the Delhi Conference at the time of his election. He was from the hill country of the Himalayan region where he was born in an isolated village. His father was a religious man but not a member of the church. Bishop Singh was the fourth native of India to be elected to the episcopacy. Upon his election he was assigned to the Bombay area where he remained until 1964. He was then assigned to the Delhi area, which he served until retirement in 1968.

Bishop Singh was a gentle soul, who had a reputation for wanting to be helpful to other people. He was well-educated, having not only studied in several institutions in India but also in the United States as a Crusade Scholar.

The bishop's administration was a pastoral one. He attended the meetings of the Council of Bishops about once a year and enjoyed the fellowship, but he rarely spoke out.

Upon his retirement Bishop Singh made his home in Bareilly, and not long afterward he lost his wife to whom he was deeply devoted. The shock of her going was more than his sensitive nature could bear, and it eventually took its toll on his health. Bishop Singh died in 1981 as the council was gathering for its spring session of that year.

GABRIEL SUNDARAM

Bishop Gabriel Sundaram was elected by the 1956 Southern Asia Central Conference. He was at the time executive secretary of Christian education for the Central Conference of Southern Asia. He was assigned to the Lucknow area.

Bishop Sundaram is a well-poised man with a reputation for being able to keep cool in the midst of a heated discussion and to say the right thing at the right time. He is a clear thinker and a good writer who has written articles for *The Indian Witness*.

A well-educated man the bishop spent almost all his ministry in the field of Christian education. For sixteen years he was headmaster of the Methodist Boys High School in Hyderabad. Previous to that he had been a teacher there for ten years.

Exhibiting a great interest in the wider church, Bishop Sundaram represented the Methodism of India in numerous ecumenical gatherings, including the Madras Conference, the Delhi Assembly of the World Council of Churches, and the World Methodist Conference at Oxford.

Following retirement Bishop Sundaram made his home in Hyderabad and continued his interest in the affairs of the church. He could not attend the 1980 General Conference of The United Methodist Church, but he was able to attend the first General Conference of the new Methodist Church in India held in Madras in 1981. He rejoiced greatly that the church in India had become an autonomous church, and he predicted that this step would lead ultimately to further church union in India.

Bishop Sundaram was able to be present at the meeting of the Council of Bishops at Rapid City, South Dakota, in the spring of 1981. The bishops had not seen him for several years.

PRINCE ALBERT TAYLOR

Bishop Prince Albert Taylor was elected by the 1956 Central Jurisdictional Conference from the editorship of the *Central Christian Advocate*. He was one of a number of bishops elected from this position, including Bishops R. E. Jones, Shaw, Brooks, Bowen, and Allen. He was an alumnus of Gammon and for a time a faculty member. For his doctoral dissertation he wrote "A History of Gammon Theological Seminary." His first episcopal assignment was to Liberia where he served for eight years. He was highly appreciated in that country and was a close friend of President W. V. Tubman and other major leaders. In 1964, as the first merger of jurisdictions and conferences began, he became a part of the Northeastern Jurisdiction. He served the New Jersey area until his retirement in 1976.

The bishop's keen, incisive mind enables him to see the implications of a decision and where it might ultimately lead. He is ready to come to the defense of the rights of his people or of persons who he thinks have suffered injustice. Usually he took a seat on the front row at the council meetings, and he was quick to arise in protest against whatever he judged unwise or wrong. He is fair in spirit and attitude toward members of his own race and to white brothers and sisters. His endeavoring to be fair and objective caused him to be censured sometimes during the extreme tensions that marked the sixties. Throughout those difficult days, he maintained his fine sense of balance and thus made an invaluable contribution.

Bishop Taylor was a very familiar figure on the United Methodist world stage. During the days that he was resident in Liberia he was often charged by the council with the responsibility of visiting other African countries where great issues of church and state were at stake. When Africa was throwing off the yoke of colonialism and new nations were being born in a day, he was a most helpful envoy shuttling back and forth in the name of the church. His close friendship with President Tubman gave him entree that was unusually valuable. After his assignment to the New Jersey area, he continued to be sent back to Liberia and other African nations on special assignment.

Bishop Taylor provided churchwide leadership at three particular points. The first was in the achievement of desegregation. He worked toward this end quietly but steadily. Some people thought him not sufficiently belligerent, but this did not deter him. He wrote position papers, engaged in dialogue, and served as a member of various strategy groups. He knew how to make the most of shared conversation to reach a conclusion, and he often added flavor or drove his point home by way of his rich sense of humor. He was the first of the bishops who had seen service in the former Central Jurisdiction to be assigned to an area made up of predominantly white conferences. Bishop James S. Thomas, newly elected by the Central Jurisdiction, was also assigned the same year by the North Central Jurisdictional Conference to predominantly white conferences, but he had not seen any years of service as a Central Jurisdictional bishop.

The second point at which Bishop Taylor took leadership in the church-at-large was as president of the Commission on Structure of Methodism Overseas from 1968 to 1972. This represented a demanding task and had far-reaching effects for United Methodism, since it involved the partial dismantling of what had long been a world church. Some former sections of United Methodism now became related autonomous churches or went into united churches, because they judged it necessary for reasons of further church development or greater national acceptance.

The third point at which Bishop Taylor took leadership in the church-at-large was the World Methodist Council; he was executive committee chairman from 1971 to 1976. Bishop Taylor was the first black to serve as president of the Council of Bishops, serving from 1965 to 1966. He used to say he was not a black bishop, but a bishop who was black. For a number of years, due to his editorial experience, he was called upon to serve as press representative of the council.

When Bishop Taylor was assigned to the New Jersey area, he chose Princeton as his residence. He has continued to live there since his retirement in 1976.

RALPH TAYLOR ALTON

Bishop Ralph Taylor Alton was elected by the 1960 North Central Jurisdictional Conference. He was at the time a pastor in Wisconsin. Previously he had spent his ministry in the North East Ohio Conference, where his father began his ministry. Later his father transferred to the Ohio Conference of which he was long a highly respected leading member. He was from 1948 to 1956 a member of the Judicial Council. Bishop Alton served the Wisconsin area for twelve years and then the Indiana area until his retirement in 1980.

Bishop Alton is a thoughtful man fully aware of the power

involved in the episcopal office, but he has remained firm in his conviction that power of this or any other kind should not be abused. He has continued to be unaffected in manner and democratic in spirit. He is a good singer, and he knows and loves the great hymns of the church.

Bishop Alton belongs to the liberal school of thought. He values the best in the past, but at the same time he favors change when it is necessary. To him, even long-cherished things ought to be subject to continuing review. He is firmly committed to the social application of the gospel. The elimination of racism is a matter of major concern to him, and as an active bishop he worked untiringly toward that end. He is an ecumenist by nature, willing to go farther in ecumenical experimentation and planning than perhaps some of his companion bishops.

Bishop Alton has a judicial mind. In council meetings he could be counted upon to know the *Discipline*, and he was skilled in its interpretation. Apparently he inherited some of his father's judicial gifts. The bishop also knew parliamentary law. He was generally acknowledged to be one of the best presiding officers among the bishops, and often he was called to take the chair in sessions that might become tough for the presiding officer. In the chair he maintained his poise, kept the parliamentary situation clear, and moved the business of the conference with dispatch.

The bishop's obvious gifts were recognized as he was called upon to be for one period the president of the Board of Hospitals and Homes and for another the president of the Board of Higher Education. From 1964 to 1972 he was president of the Methodist Committee on Overseas Relief.

Bishop Alton served as secretary of the Council of Bishops from 1972 to 1976, and he sought carefully to improve its procedures. He had had previous secretarial experience in his earlier ministry when for some years he was the secretary of the large Ohio Conference.

He served as president of the Council of Bishops from 1979 to 1980. He and Bishops H. Lester Smith and G. Bromley Oxnam were the only ones to serve as both secretary and president of the council.

Bishop Alton rounded out his active episcopacy by being the host bishop to the 1980 General Conference, which met in Indianapolis.

Following retirement Bishop and Mrs. Alton moved again to Madison, Wisconsin, where the bishop became a member of the staff of a local church.

PAUL V. GALLOWAY

Bishop Paul V. Galloway was elected by the 1960 South Central Jurisdictional Conference from the pastorate of Boston Avenue Church, Tulsa, Oklahoma, where he had served for ten years. Previous to his Tulsa pastorate he had served churches in the two Arkansas Conferences. Boston Avenue Church had seen a former pastor, Bishop H. Bascom Watts, elected before Bishop Galloway and later was to see three of its pastors in a row after him elected to the episcopacy. They were Bishops Finis A. Crutchfield, J. Chess Lovern, and John W. Russell.

Bishop Galloway was a product of the parsonage, his father having served for many years as a pastor in Arkansas. It is interesting to note that not only Bishop Galloway but all five bishops elected by the 1960 South Central Jurisdictional Conference were pastors at the time.

Bishop Galloway was asigned to the newly formed San Antonio area which he served for four years. In 1964 he was assigned to the Arkansas area where he served until retirement in 1972.

The bishop has a generous heart, and the sufferings of others move him deeply. His sympathy has often found expression in concrete action. The bishop has been exceedingly popular with laymen. His down-to-earthness forthrightness, humanness, and outgoing personality win admiration wherever he goes.

There is no pretense about Bishop Galloway. He speaks his mind freely and honestly. He tends toward conservative theological and social views but not ultraconservative ones. He loves the Methodist Church and feels strongly about anything that might impair its effectiveness or hurt its influence. He found some of the pressures upon the church, particularly in the sixties, difficult to take, and he did not hesitate to voice his reaction.

The bishop is a genuine evangelist. He knows how to win people for Christ, and in doing that he has had his greatest joy. As a pastor he sought to make his churches evangelistic, and in the episcopacy he sought to do the same thing with his conferences. Following his retirement he became associated with the staff of the General Board of Evangelism and traveled throughout the country on evangelistic missions.

Early in the 1972-1976 quadrennium Bishop Copeland died, and Bishop Galloway was called out of retirement to serve the Houston area. He kept this assignment to the end of the quadrennium. When Bishop Shamblin died he took over the Louisiana Area in 1983 for the remainder of the quadrennium. On retirement he and Mrs. Galloway made their home first in Little Rock, Arkansas, and later in Tulsa, Oklahoma.

EDWIN R. GARRISON

Bishop Edwin R. Garrison was elected by the 1960 North Central Jurisdictional Conference. He was at the time the administrative assistant to Bishop Richard C. Raines of the Indiana area. He came of a family well represented in the Methodist ministry of Indiana, Illinois, and Ohio. He was a popular son of the Indiana Conference where he had served as pastor and district superintendent and in the area office. He was assigned to the Dakotas area where he served until his retirement in 1968.

Bishop Garrison is a thoughtful man who ponders carefully the issues and the problems that demand his attention. He is all-business and fully committed to his tasks.

Bishop Garrison is primarily a pastor with a heart and a pastor's devotion. His emphasis has been upon the local church—perhaps more than any other bishop in his day. He served the Dakotas area with its vast distances and its many smaller churches as a pastor-bishop. He let nothing come before his area, and he shuttled back and forth across the two large states with unwearying devotion.

The bishop also has special interest in church structure. Prior to his election he had been a valuable member of the Coordinating Council. The year he was elected bishop he was also elected president of the Coordinating Council. One of the functions of that council, which had its existence from 1952 to 1972, was to study the functioning of the church and make recommendations for improvement. The leadership of Bishop Garrison, was invaluable at this point. Always he was the careful, cautious leader, respecting the past but at the same time committed to what might prove to be constructive change. During his presidency the Coordinating Council carried forward a study of the episcopacy and made recommendations to the 1964 General Conference. Those who know the story know how largely the widsom of Bishop Garrison was represented in what proved to be most helpful in this report.

The Coordinating Council had no easy responsibilities assigned to it, and at times it had to encounter sharp reactions to its exercise of the leadership the church desired from it. When any sharp reaction came, the bishop would maintain a steady poise that would contribute significantly toward the solution of the problem.

At the request of the Council of Bishops, upon retirement Bishop Garrison made a study of the parish. The active bishops made large use of his findings in their respective areas. The impression made by this study was such that Bishop Garrison was invited to teach a regular course in Duke Divinity School for several years.

Following his teaching assignment at Duke, Bishop and Mrs. Garrison have made their home at Englewood, Florida, in the winter and at Franklin, Indiana, in the summer.

CHARLES F. GOLDEN

Bishop Charles F. Golden was elected by the 1960 Central Jurisdictional Conference. In his earlier ministry he had served as a pastor, a teacher, and a chaplain in World War II. At the time of his election he was one of the secretaries of the National Division of the Board of Missions, occupying a similar post to that from which Bishops W. A. C. Hughes and

The Episcopal Leadership Team 1940–1967

Edgar A. Love were elected before him. He was assigned to the newly created Nashville-Birmingham area which included the Central Jurisdiction work in Tennessee, Alabama, and South Carolina, and later in Kentucky. He served this area until the abolition of the Central Jurisdiction in 1968. At that time as the former Evangelical United Brethren bishops and the Central Jurisdiction bishops were allocated among the geographic jurisdiction, he was assigned to the Western Jurisdiction. There he served the San Francisco area from 1968 to 1972 and then the Los Angeles area until his retirement in 1980.

Bishop Golden is proud of his African heritage. He is a son of the parsonage; his father, Dr. J. W. Golden, was a leader widely known in Methodism who spent the last years of his ministry as one of the secretaries of the Board of Evangelism. It was one of the great joys of the old gentleman's life that he lived to see his son elected to the episcopacy.

Bishop Golden feels deeply the oppression of his people and the indignities suffered by them. A strong defender of the rights of his people, he was quick to rise to his feet in protest at council meetings when he felt it necessary. On such occasions he could speak sharp words to drive his point home. He has been an advocate of the elimination of segregation structures from the life of the church, and during the sixties when this was being attempted, he served on a number of committees and task forces set up for this purpose. As the final integration of the jurisdictions and Annual Conferences got under way, he maintained a monitoring position, seeking to protect the concerns of his people.

Bishop Golden was a firm administrator who kept in full command of his conferences. He sometimes gave an impression of being rather quick in making decisions, but he did not hesitate to reverse a decision if he was given sufficient reason.

The Council of Bishops honored Bishop Golden by electing him president in 1973. The bishop's last quadrennium as an active bishop was an exceedingly taxing one for him because his Pacific-Southwest Conference became involved in a lawsuit over one of its philanthropic institutions, the Pacific

Homes, a suit that came to involve the whole United Methodist Church. Bishop Golden necessarily became a focal point in the situation and found the strain almost too overwhelming. Retirement came to him as a relief.

Following retirement, Bishop and Mrs. Golden have continued to make their home in Los Angeles.

PAUL HARDIN, JR.

Bishop Paul Hardin, Jr., was elected by the 1960 Southeastern Jurisdictional Conference. At the time he was pastor of First Church, Birmingham, Alabama. He had grown up in the South Carolina Conference, but his earlier ministry had been spent in the Western North Carolina Conference. He was a close friend of Bishop John W. Branscomb and Bishop Edward J. Pendergrass, and the three of them together with Dr. Mack Anthony had composed a gospel quartet when they were students at Candler School of Theology.

Bishop Hardin was assigned to the newly created Columbia area composed of his home conference. The first responsibility he faced was filling Bethel Church, Charleston, from which Bishop John Owen Smith had just been elected to the episcopacy. The first appointment involved the placing of his brother in this significant pulpit. The bishop was apologetic about filling the vacancy from his family, but the conference understood well that this first appointment was made objectively. The bishop served the Columbia area for his entire active episcopacy, retiring in 1972. Following the death of Bishop Hodge, he cared for the Alabama-West Florida Conference for three years.

Bishop Hardin is a matter-of-fact person, who speaks his mind freely and crisply. His good business sense makes him fully at home in the realm of practical affairs. The church recognized this ability when it made him the president of the Council on World Service and Finance for four years.

Bishop Hardin is a popular preacher. For eleven years he filled acceptably the Birmingham pulpit which earlier had been filled by such giants as George R. Stuart and Arthur J. Moore. Throughout his active episcopacy he was in demand for preaching engagements throughout the church, and in his retirement the demand continues.

Bishop Hardin contributed at the area level to the solution of problems incident to the elimination of the Central Jurisdiction. There was a larger concentration of black Methodists in South Carolina than anywhere else in the church, and there were, of course, some deep-seated southern traditions in this state where the first shots of the Civil War had been fired. Bishop Hardin moved in upon the integration of the two conferences with fairness and firmness that won the appreciation of South Carolina blacks and whites alike and commanded the admiration of the entire church.

Bishop Hardin was the president of the Council of Bishops from 1971 to 1972.

Upon retiring, Bishop and Mrs. Hardin moved to Lake Junaluska, North Carolina, a place that they have long loved. There the bishop continues to participate enthusiastically in the affairs of the assembly, to share in the life of nearby congregations, and to make his way to the golf links almost every day except the Lord's day.

Bishop Hardin has the distinction of being the presiding bishop for all his active episcopacy of the Annual Conference (South Carolina) of which he in his beginning ministry, his grant-grandfather, the Reverend T. E. Wannamaker, and his great-great-grandfather, the Reverend R. J. Boyd, had all been members.

JAMES W. HENLEY

Bishop James W. Henley was elected by the 1960 Southeastern Jurisdictional Conference. He was at the time pastor of West End Church, Nashville, from which pulpit sixteen years before Bishop Costen J. Harrell had been elected and from which twenty years later Bishop Roy C. Clark would be elected. Bishop Henley spent his beginning ministry in the Holston Conference. He was somewhat of a protégé of Bishop William N. Ainsworth. His next bishop, Paul Kern, also felt he was a minister with whom large responsibility could be lodged. He was assigned to the Florida area, which he served until his retirement in 1972.

Bishop Henley is outgoing and makes friends easily. At heart he is a devoted pastor. That was the strength of his ministry in the years prior to his election. He did a greater than average amount of visiting for a pastor of a large church. He paid particular attention to the sick, the sorrowing, and the prospects for membership. He could help his people feel a sense of their importance as individuals.

As a bishop, Bishop Henley continued to take a pastoral approach. His area was his world, and he loved it. He gave full attention to every detail. He cultivated and depended upon his cabinet, but at the same time he recognized the final responsibility which was his as a bishop and he did not hesitate to accept it. He would take his chosen stand in a quiet manner, at times making some brief explanation, but he would stand firm and not retreat. His ministry in Florida came at a time of large expansion in that state, and he sought to keep Florida Methodism in step with what was happening there.

Bishop Henley regularly attended the meetings of the council, but he seldom took the floor. He was cordial with all the bishops, delighting especially in conversations in the halls at recess time and in meals shared together. Much that he wanted to say he got in at such times.

Bishop Henley retired in 1972. He and Mrs. Henley continue to make their home in Lakeland, Florida. He became connected with an educational tour organization in which capacity he has traveled extensively and has arranged various overseas trips and educational experiences for a number of bishops and their people.

FRED G. HOLLOWAY

Bishop Fred G. Holloway was elected by the 1960 Northeastern Jurisdictional Conference. He was at the time president of Drew Seminary and previously had been president of both Westminster Theological Seminary and Western Maryland. He was the first bishop with a Methodist Protestant background to be elected in the twenty-one-year period after Methodist union. Interestingly enough, another bishop with a Methodist Protestant background, Kenneth Copeland, was elected the same year by the South Central

Jurisdictional Conference. Bishop Holloway was assigned to the newly created West Virginia area, which he served until retirement in 1968.

Bishop Holloway's rich sense of humor expresses itself in keen observations in his preaching, casual conversation, and sometimes in a bit of humorous, freshly written poetry provoked by some situation to which he has reacted.

Bishop Holloway belongs in the category of the scholar in the episcopacy. He has read extensively, and whatever he has written, whether a general article or a position paper, has been marked by exactness, logic, and polish. He loves great poetry and has himself the poet's touch. On occasion he would write humorous jingles, but he also could produce higher quality poetry. He knows beauty of language and is a master in word painting. One of the unforgettable social occasions for members of the council came at its meeting in Charleston, West Virginia, the spring following his retirement, when he was the featured speaker and brought a message on the religious contribution of great poetry.

For much of his career Bishop Holloway was an educator, and he continued this interest in the years of his episcopacy. He has been committed to the full support of church-related institutions of higher education. He believes in a well-trained ministry and has made significant contributions toward the training of such a ministry. When he was bishop of West Virginia, where there are many small churches, he sought to find an adequate ministry for them by enlisting trained ministers, grouping churches to provide a more challenging working situation, and developing a more adequate financial support basis.

Bishop Holloway was a most interesting member of the Council of Bishops. He was never an officer, but no one followed its proceedings with greater care. He was one member of the council of whom it could be said that all the bishops were happy when he took the floor, because what he said was usually brief and somewhat humorous. He had the capacity to puncture ecclesiastical balloons with rare skill, and he found amusement in doing that.

When Bishop Holloway retired, the educational world

called once again, and he assumed teaching responsibilities at Morris Harvey College at Barbourville, West Virginia. There he taught for several years, but eventually he and Mrs. Holloway moved to Wilmington, Delaware, to make their home.

JAMES K. MATHEWS

Bishop James K. Mathews was elected by the 1960 Northeastern Jurisdictional Conference. At the time he was secretary of the World Division of the Board of Missions. His membership was in the New York Conference. He has the distinction of twice being elected a bishop; no other bishop of the Methodist Church or The United Methodist Church can make this claim. Earlier he had been elected by the Central Conference of Southern Asia, but he had declined the election in favor of a national. In the Methodist Episcopal Church Bishop Joshua Soule was first elected in 1820 but did not accept election. He was elected a second time in 1824, and then he accepted the office. A similar thing happened to Bishop Atticus G. Haygood in the Methodist Episcopal Church, South, in 1882 when he declined but was again elected in 1890 when he accepted. Upon election Bishop Mathews was assigned to the Boston area, which he served until 1972. Then he was assigned to the Washington area, which he served until retirement in 1980.

Bishop Mathews is characterized by a deliberateness that stood him in good stead when he presided at a General Conference. He is a popular and convincing speaker and a good writer with several books and articles to his credit. He is liberal in thought and commitment, and his passion is to see the kingdom come upon earth.

As a young man Bishop Mathews was a missionary in India, where he became the son-in-law of the famous missionaries, Dr. and Mrs. E. Stanley Jones.

Bishop Mathews was a vocal member of the Council of Bishops. He is by nature an idea man, and many of his creative suggestions were adopted. From time to time he would present a position paper in the council to get a discussion under way. During the last four years of his active episcopacy he was the secretary of the council.

The Episcopal Leadership Team 1940-1967

Bishop Mathews has been particularly interested in fuller cooperation with the three black Methodist bodies in the United States, and it was at his initiative that arrangements were worked out, beginning in 1979, for regular consultation of all the bishops of the African Methodist Episcopal Church, the African Methodist Episcopal Church Zion, the Christian Methodist Episcopal Church, and The United Methodist Church.

Bishop Mathews has played a leadership role not only in Methodism-at-large but also in the ecumenical church. He came into the council as one already familiar with the world church. During the years he was the secretary of the World Division of the Board of Missions, he had contacts with the executives of the great world Christian bodies. He was a familiar figure in every land where the Methodist Church operated. Perhaps no bishop since 1960 has been better known in the world church than Bishop Mathews. The great leaders of the world church of recent years have been familiar figures to him and he to them. A testimony to this fact came when, as a new bishop, he entertained the Council of Bishops in Boston in 1961 and brought Dr. Willem A. Visser't Hooft from Geneva to be the speaker upon the public occasion.

Bishop Mathews served for many years on the Central Committee of the World Council of Churches, on the General Board of the National Council of Churches, and on the Consultation on Church Union. He has a strong commitment to ecumenicity, although at the same time he has a pronounced attachment to the Methodist heritage and to the basic features of Methodist polity. He believes that a case can be made for episcopacy after the Methodist pattern, and that in planning for a uniting church bringing together the various traditions, full consideration needs to be given to the idea of an episcopacy constitutionally defined.

The Methodist world church concept appealed to Bishop Mathews, and he reacted adversely to the process of dismantling that took place beginning in 1964. Perhaps no bishop was in better position to feel emotionally this dismantling than he, because of his long connection with the missionary enterprise, as both missionary and board executive.

Throughout his active episcopacy, Bishop Mathews was a voice for the World Council in the Council of Bishops as Bishop Oxnam and Bishop Baker had been before him.

Following retirement in 1980, Bishop and Mrs. Mathews have continued to make their home in Washington, D.C.

NOAH W. MOORE, JR.

Bishop Noah W. Moore, Jr., was elected by the 1960 Central Jurisdictional Conference. He was at the time pastor of the famous Tindley Temple Church in Philadelphia, which has been one of the truly great churches of Methodism. It developed into a great church under the ministry of the famous preacher, singer, and hymn writer, Dr. Charles A. Tindley, who spent a ministry of thirty-one years there. It had one hundred thirty members when his ministry began and over seven thousand when it ended. In addition it had over two thousand preparatory members and possessed a large, well-equipped church plant. Of such a church Bishop Moore was the highly effective pastor for eleven years. He was one of three bishops elected by the Central Jurisdiction in 1960. This was the largest number elected by that jurisdiction at any one time; the other bishops elected were Charles F. Golden and M. L. Harris. Bishop Moore was assigned to the New Orleans area. He served there for eight years, before he was assigned to the Nebraska area, which he served until retirement in 1972.

Bishop Moore has a becoming dignity and reserve. He is a strong defender of the rights of his people, but he entertains no bitterness of spirit. In council meetings he was adept and helpful in working out solutions to problems, and he made significant contributions in the sixties to bringing about a new Methodism without structures based upon race.

Bishop Moore is primarily a preacher, always in demand throughout the church for pulpit appearances. His style is uniquely his own. He takes a scripture passage, holds it up to the light, lets the light play upon it, and makes it shine with insight and new meaning. He is given to life-situation preaching, and he has his own inimitable way of relating biblical situations to parallels in modern life.

The Episcopal Leadership Team 1940–1967

For years Bishop and Mrs. Moore maintained a home at Atlantic City, a place that they very much loved. Following retirement, they moved back there permanently. In the early years of his retirement Bishop Moore traveled the country under the auspices of the Board of Evangelism on preaching missions.

T. OTTO NALL

Bishop T. Otto Nall was elected by the 1960 North Central Jurisdictional Conference from the editorship of *The Christian Advocate*. He was one of a long line of editors of church publications elected to the episcopacy, including fifteen elected in the Methodist Episcopal Church and seven elected in the Methodist Episcopal Church, South, prior to Methodist union in 1939; Bishops Brooks, Taylor, Allen, Harmon, and Short have been elected since Methodist union. He was a member of the Minnesota Conference and was one of the few bishops who was assigned to the area from which he was elected. He served the Minnesota area until his retirement in 1968.

Bishop Nall had a characteristic posture he always took at council meetings. He would sit near the front of the room, bending over his desk, and take careful notes on whatever was being said. Thus in the council he was still the editor working away.

Bishop Nall's editorial gifts had long been recognized by the church. He could spot a story and write it to perfection. As an editor he kept himself fully aware of all the changing issues confronting the church, and as a bishop he continued to do the same thing. As a bishop he often wrote position papers setting forth his convictions, and they were always done with thoroughness and skill.

Bishop Nall is one of only two or three bishops who were never pastors. All his early ministry was spent in editorial offices of the church where he had close associations with some of the greats of that day.

He has more rich memories of Methodism between 1918 and 1939 than perhaps any other bishop because as a young representative of the press he was on hand to witness most of the significant gatherings of those years. It is most rewarding to hear him reminisce and recall the characters and events of that period in the life of the church.

The bishop has a great interest in Methodist history and is thoroughly familiar with the story. For a quadrennium he was president of the Commission on Archives and History. In 1973 he wrote a history of Methodism in Minnesota entitled *Forever Beginning*.

Upon Bishop Nall's retirement in 1968, the council asked him to take over the Hong Kong-Taiwan area. He and Mrs. Nall moved to Hong Kong and supervised the work, culminating their efforts with the organization of the autonomous church there. Since final retirement, the Nalls, have made their home in Clearwater, Florida.

W. KENNETH POPE

Bishop W. Kenneth Pope was elected by the South Central Jurisdictional Conference of 1960. He was at the time pastor of First Church, Houston. He was a son of the parsonage, his father having served charges in Missouri, Texas, and Oklahoma. Bishop Pope started out as a boy preacher while still in school. As a young preacher he was an ardent evangelist, holding many revival meetings. He lived to witness the decline of the revival meeting but continued an evangelistic emphasis throughout his career.

When he was tempted as a young preacher to launch immediately into a full-time evangelistic career, Bishop Paul Kern, then the dean of SMU (Southern Methodist University), convinced him that an effective ministry must be a prepared ministry. He heeded this advice and not only finished at SMU but also went on to the Yale Graduate School of Religion for three years. Bishop John M. Moore was particularly appreciative of his gifts and ministry and appointed him to several churches in Texas and Missouri. Bishop Frank Smith took him to First Church, Austin, and from there he was sent to First Church, Houston, following the death of Dr. Paul Quillian, its very popular pastor.

Upon his election Bishop Pope was assigned to the

Arkansas area where he served until going to the Dallas area in 1964. He served the Dallas area until his retirement in 1972.

Bishop Pope's alert mind can grasp a situation without delay. He seems to have an absorbing interest in whatever is going on, and, he does not hesitate to ask questions.

The bishop has been a vigorous preacher. His sermons not only have basic content but also are replete with observations and illustrative material to keep his listeners' attention. Throughout his episcopacy he continued the pulpit emphasis that made him the pastor of great churches.

Bishop Pope adopted in young manhood the habit of seeking to hear and to get to know people who had something to give—great speakers, great teachers, and great artists. A list of such persons, written by his hand, testifies dramatically to his success at this point. He seeks opportunities for enriching experiences, and to this end he plans to be on hand for great church assemblies or significant public occasions. He also seeks such opportunities through travel, and his travels have covered the globe itself.

Bishop Pope regularly took a seat on the front or second row in the meetings of the Council of Bishops. There he would listen carefully to everything being said. Occasionally he would take the floor to enter into some discussion, usually introducing his remarks through a provocative question. He was never an officer of the council, a fact which apparently held no disappointment for him.

Since retirement Bishop and Mrs. Pope have continued to live in Dallas, where for four years he was bishop in residence at Perkins School of Theology. During his retirement years he has published an account of his career under the interesting title, *A Pope at Roam*.

O. EUGENE SLATER

Bishop O. Eugene Slater was elected by the 1960 South Central Jurisdictional Conference from the pastorate of Polk Street Church, Amarillo, Texas. He was a favorite son of Texas and had served in three of the Texas Conferences. He enjoyed a close and long connection with Southern Methodist University, taking both his undergraduate and his theological work there, serving for some years as a member of its Board of Trustees, and in his retirement becoming bishop in residence for a quadrennium. He was assigned to the Kansas area, which he served until 1964. He then went to the San Antonio area, where he remained until his retirement in 1976.

Bishop Slater's nature is reflected in his movements, speech, and countenance. He is ever the considerate Christian gentleman. Any assignment given him by the council was done with thoroughness, but he participated in the floor debates only to a limited extent. He served as the president of the council from 1972 to 1973.

During the years that Bishop Slater had the San Antonio area, the Rio Grand Conference was a part of that area. Thus the larger part of the Spanish work of Methodism in the United States was under his supervision for twelve years. He was devoted to this work, and he conscientiously advocated the concerns of the Hispanic minority in the church.

Bishop Slater has been involved in the work of Methodism in Korea. At the request of the Council of Bishops he took over from Bishop Werner the liaison responsibility with Korean Methodism. He carried this responsibility for some years—years which proved to be difficult for both Korea and the Korean Methodist Church. The bishop gave continuing wise counsel and kept the channels open between the Korean Church and United Methodism as a whole. He made a number of trips to the Far East in the discharge of this responsibility. The Koreans held him in highest appreciation.

Another of Bishop Slater's interests has been Methodist history. He served form 1972 to 1976 as president of the Commission on Archives and History.

Bishop Slater retired in 1976, and he and Mrs. Slater moved to Dallas, Texas. There he became Bishop in residence at Perkins School of Theology. In his later retirement years Bishop Slater has continued his lifelong interest in world travel.

W. RALPH WARD

Bishop W. Ralph Ward was elected by the 1960 Northeastern Jurisdictional Conference from the pastorate of Mount

The Episcopal Leadership Team 1940–1967

Lebanon Church, Pittsburgh, the same church from which Bishop Wicke had been elected twelve years before. Previously he has held pastorates in Maine, Massachusetts, Rhode Island, and Connecticut. He was the second Ralph Ward to be elected to the episcopacy; the other was Bishop Ralph A. Ward, elected by the 1937 China Central Conference, who died in 1958.

Bishop Ward was assigned to the Syracuse area, which he served for twelve years. He was then assigned to the New York area, which he served until retirement in 1980.

Bishop Ward is a liberal without apology, but his is not an intolerant liberalism. He accords to others the right to entertain opinions that differ from his own. He speaks his convictions freely and is unafraid of whatever reaction their expression might invite. He has a quiet, matter-of-fact, sometimes almost offhand way of saying what he has to say. One of the bishop's outstanding characteristics is his obvious fairness which evidenced itself in his administration and his ability to preside.

Bishop Ward has a strong social conscience. He believes the church should minister to the whole man, including his environment. Every social problem that has represented injustice to or exploitation of persons has been a matter of concern to him. He is the friend and defender of all God's children, especially those who stand in greatest need of a friend and defender. Since he is such a socially concerned person, it is not surprising that the Fund for Reconciliation approved by the 1968 General Conference was originally very largely his brainchild. It is his habit to keep looking to the future, and he is not afraid of experimentation or change.

Bishop Ward was one of the bishops most active in the meetings of the council, and he participated effectively in discussions. He undertook numerous special assignments for the council, and he prepared a number of the position papers that helped set it on a new course of action. From 1968 to 1972 he was president of the Program Council, which had been a familiar pattern to those coming out of the Evangelical United Brethren tradition but which was an entirely new concept to those coming out of the Methodist tradition. From 1975 to 1976 he served as president of the Council of Bishops.

Following retirement in 1980, Bishop and Mrs. Ward made their home at Convent Station, New Jersey, and he became bishop in residence at Drew University. For a period he served temporarily as associate general secretary of the World Division of the Board of Global Ministries, pending on election to fill the office.

PEDRO R. ZOTTELE

Bishop Pedro R. Zottele was elected by the 1962 Latin American Central Conference. He had been a teacher and a pastor in Chile for some years. Upon his election he was assigned to the Pacific area where he followed Bishop Sabanes who had been forced to retire because of illness. The Pacific area included the work in Costa Rica, Panama, Peru, and Chile, which meant it covered the entire west coast of South America and was both the longest and the narrowest area in the entire church. Bishop Zottele faithfully traveled this greatly expanded area until his retirement in 1969.

An enthusiastic advocate of evangelism, Bishop Zottele is an effective evangelist. His great desire is to witness the conversion of individuals and the building up of the church. He is conservative in his theological and social views. Frequently he would rise in the Council of Bishops to plead for understanding of the situation in both the state and the church in the countries of his area.

Bishop Zottele is an inveterate traveler. Practically all travel in his area involved long distances. He also went to Central Conference and ecumenical meetings of one character or another throughout Latin America. He usually made the meetings of the Council of Bishops, though often he was the bishop having to travel the farthest.

Bishop Zottele was the son-in-law of Bishop Roberto Elphick, and the two of them together gave twelve years of episcopal service in the same Pacific Area.

As Bishop Zottele came to retirement, he saw the churches of the countries where he had served become autonomous or enter into unions. This movement had his blessing. He was host to the final session of the Latin American Central Conference in Santiago in 1969.

The Episcopal Leadership Team 1940–1967

In retirement Bishop Zottele lives in Santiago and serves a small church in a very poor section where he developed a social service program. Bishop Elphick before him had followed this same pattern. Bishop Zottele continues a member of the Council of Bishops and attends its meetings with some frequency.

HARRY P. ANDREASSEN

Bishop Harry P. Andreassen was elected by the 1964 Africa Central Conference. He was a native of Norway who, after a period of service as an evangelist and as a pastor in his own country, had gone to Africa as a missionary in 1952. At the time of his election he was a missionary in Angola, and his assignment was to the Angola area. He was elected as a term bishop. He was reelected in 1968 but was not reelected in 1972. He then returned to Norway to resume his ministry there.

Bishop Andreassen's years in Africa were at a time of great conflict and stress. The Portuguese yoke was being thrown off, and a new nation was being born. Bishop Andreassen was careful about what positions he took and about what he said publicly. He loves the church and was reluctant to take any position he thought might endanger its ability to maintain its ministry. He was able to attend only a few meetings of the Council of Bishops, because he experienced difficulty in getting travel documents.

Bishops Andreassen has two distinctions. First of all, he was the last of the long line of white bishops serving in Africa that included Bishops William Taylor, Joseph C. Hartzell, Walter R. Lambuth, Eben S. Johnson, John Springer, Newell Booth, and Ralph E. Dodge. Second, he was one of that all-too-often overlooked noble company of missionaries sent to the far corners of the earth from the conferences of the Methodist Church in Europe.

H. ELLIS FINGER, JR.

Bishop H. Ellis Finger, Jr., was elected by the 1964 Southeastern Jurisdictional Conference. He was at the time president of Millsaps College at Jackson, Mississippi. He was a member of the North Mississippi Conference, and he remains the one member of that conference elected to the episcopacy so far. He had been a chaplain during World War II, and before going to Millsaps where he had a twelve-year presidency, he had served in several pastorates. He was assigned to the Nashville area, which at that time was composed of the Tennessee, Memphis, and Holston Conferences and was the largest area in the church. In 1968 the Holston Conference became a separate area, and the bishop was left with the Memphis and Tennessee Conferences. He served these two conferences until 1976 when he was sent to the Holston area, where he was returned in 1980. He thus served the whole of the original Nashville area for four years, two-thirds of it for eight years and one-third for eight years.

Bishop Finger was all-business. He was sparing in words and tended to carry his responsibilities with marked seriousness. He had a gift for analysis and was able to size up a situation with alacrity.

Bishop Finger is conscientious to a fine point and stresses integrity. Although he came out of a conservative section, he has insisted upon looking to the future. He has worked diligently for the overcoming of racial barriers, for giving to women every privilege of the church, and for recognizing the claims of minorities for proper consideration.

Bishop Finger is committed to Christian education. As a young pastor he served Oxford University Methodist Church, Oxford, Mississippi. For twelve years he was the president of Millsaps, one of United Methodism's great schools. For twelve years he was the president of the Board of Trustees of Scarritt College. As a bishop his interest continued in education. He felt that the Council of Bishops meetings should include some educational experience. He was one of the bishops who took the lead in arranging for the periodic appearances at council meetings of outstanding scholars to lecture on latest developments in their chosen fields.

The church soon learned that Bishop Finger could be trusted with responsibility at the general church level. For four years it asked him to be the president of the Council on

Finance and Administration. From 1981 to 1982 he was the president of the Council of Bishops.

W. KENNETH GOODSON

Bishop W. Kenneth Goodson was elected by the 1964 Southeastern Jurisdictional Conference. He was at the time pastor of Centenary Church, Winston-Salem, North Carolina. All his ministry had been spent in the Western North Carolina Conference. He was assigned to the Birmingham area, which he served for eight years. Following that he served the Richmond area for eight years until his retirement in 1980.

Bishop Goodson could roll with the punches. He had a rich sense of humor which reflected itself constantly in his preaching, his side remarks when presiding, his participation in debate and discussion, and his casual conversation. His humor sometimes took the form of playfulness, and there was forever something of the boy about him. He could quash a matter quickly with a humorous remark that was packed with a wallop. He could also be direct, and forthright, and bold when the occasion demanded. He was intensely interested in whatever was going on, and his nature was such that he could never be content with a mere spectator role. It was natural for him to get into things, and in the language of the world of affairs he knew his way around. It was normal for him to be in the middle of whatever was happening unless it was something in which he was totally uninterested.

Bishop Goodson usually took a seat on the back row at council meetings with three or four bishops to whom he felt close and whose company he enjoyed. Though a back row bishop as far as his choice of a seat was concerned, he was a front row bishop as far as his participation in council affairs was concerned.

A highly popular preacher, Bishop Goodson has attracted large audiences wherever he goes. His preaching is biblical, warm, fervent, evangelistic, dramatic, and deeply moving at times. It is alive with telling illustrations and illuminating observations.

The bishop proved to be adept at dealing with difficult problems and seeking their resolutions. He did not ask to be excused when the going was rough. He was the bishop of Alabama at the time of the Selma march. The governor of the state, George Wallace, was a Methodist. When the situation arose, the bishop immediately contacted the governor as his chief pastor and urged him to do what was sensible and right. He hastened to Selma so that he could have some part in resolving the crisis. In 1968 when the dissolution of the Central Jurisdiction came, he was still the bishop of Alabama, and he addressed himself creatively to the integration of conferences in what had long been the heart of the Old South. He was the first chairman of the Commission on Religion and Race from 1968 to 1972. Bishop Goodson was president of the Council of Bishops from 1976 to 1977.

One of his major concerns has been the local church. His great dream for every local church is for it to become evangelistic in outreach, contributing to the spiritual growth of persons. This was his passion as a pastor and a district superintendent, and it continued as a bishop administering an area. It is not surprising, therefore, that he should have been chosen during the last eight years of his active episcopacy to be the president of the Board of Discipleship.

Bishop Goodson retired in 1980, and he and Mrs. Goodson made their home in Durham, North Carolina, where he became bishop in residence of Duke University.

EARL G. HUNT, JR.

Bishop Earl G. Hunt, Jr., was elected by the 1964 Southeastern Jurisdictional Conference. At the time he was the president of Emory and Henry College. Prior to his presidency he had held pastorates at Morristown and Chattanooga, Tennessee. He was a favorite son of the Holston Conference. Before Methodist union in 1939 the Holston country had been border territory with both the Methodist Episcopal Church and the Methodist Episcopal Church, South, represented in many communities. The Holston Conference of the Methodist Episcopal Church was one of the strongest conferences of that church in the South. Bishop Hunt grew up in First Church, Johnson City, a congregation of that conference. He was the only bishop elected by the Southeastern Jurisdiction to come originally out of a Methodist Episcopal background. He was assigned to the Charlotte area where he served for twelve years. In 1976 he was assigned to the Nashville area and in 1980 to the Florida area.

The bishop is a giant of a man intellectually as well as physically. He has a penetrating mind and an unsual ability to organize and express his thoughts. He is an omnivorous reader.

The bishop is a gentle, kind person. He wants everybody to be happy, and he laboured to that impossible end as an administrator. By nature he does not relish tough decison making, but he accepted that as a necessary part of the episcopal office and did not flinch from it.

Bishop Hunt is generally acknowledged as one of the strongest preachers among the bishops. The pulpit is his throne. His sermons are carefully thought out. He is a master at diction, and in his preparation he labors over every word to be sure it says exactly what he wants to say. He has an appreciation of the poetic, and his discourses have a strange musical rhythm, flow, and beauty. His staccato delivery is forceful with the driving power of conviction. He is a natural choice as the preacher for momentous occasions; he delivered the keynote address at the World Methodist Council at Dublin, Ireland, in 1973.

A major interest is Christian education. Bishop Hunt had given eight years of his life to this cause at Emory and Henry. As a bishop he showed particular concern for the educational institutions of his area and devoted a great deal of time and attention to them. He has supported the idea of continuing education for ministers, and he developed the pattern of areawide conferences on preaching as a unique contribution to this end. His natural committee choice in the council was the Committee on Teaching Concerns. In line with this long continuing interest, in 1980 he was elected the president of the Board of Higher Education and Ministry.

FRANCIS E. KEARNS

Bishop Francis E. Kearns was elected by the 1964 North Central Jurisdictional Conference. He was at the time pastor of First Church, Wauwatosa, Wisconsin. Before that Bishop

Kearns had served pastorates in the Pittsburgh and Ohio Conferences. He was assigned to the East Ohio area with residence at Canton. He continued as the bishop of this area until his retirement in 1976.

Bishop Kearns is known for his graciousness, kindness, and consideration. For twelve years he was the treasurer of the bishop's Courtesy Fund, having the responsibility to remember birthdays and anniversaries and to send flowers to episcopal family members in case of illness or death. This responsibility accorded fully with Bishop Kearns's thoughtful nature, and he carried it to perfection.

Bishop Kearns is a well-trained man with two Ph.D. degrees, one from the University of Pittsburgh and the other from Baldwin-Wallace. He has done occasional writing, and he writes well. In the 1972–1976 quadrennium he chaired for the council a committee to develop an evangelistic message to the church. He gave himself with diligence to this assignment, and the paper finally developed reflected not only his writing talent but also his ability to enlist the services of others, particularly of scholars of renown.

Bishop Kearn's major interest was his episcopal area. He made his regular assigned episcopal visits to various parts of the world and took his proper share of work on general boards and agencies of the church, but that to which he gave his fullest attention and devotion was the ongoing work of his own area.

Bishop Kearns retired in 1976, and he and Mrs. Kearns moved to Delaware, Ohio, where the bishop began a teaching ministry at Ohio Seminary.

DWIGHT E. LODER

Bishop Dwight E. Loder was elected by the 1964 North Central Jurisdictional Conference. He was at the time president of Garrett Seminary. Previously he had served in the Central New York Conference and had been pastor of Hennepin Avenue Church, Minneapolis, from whose pulpit Bishop Richard C. Raines and several other pastors had been elected to the episcopacy. He was assigned to the Detroit area where he remained until being transferred to the West Ohio area in 1976.

The Episcopal Leadership Team 1940–1967

The bishop has a unique preaching style. He uses biblical passages, but his interpretations of them often contain an element of surprise. He relates the ancient passages in his own way to the current situation and thus gives them freshness. He also refers frequently to the works of modern authors and to current significant events. The passion in his delivery urges the acceptance of his message that is often strongly hortatory.

The bishop has an interest in the ministry and theological education, which is to be expected since he spent a significant part of his career training preachers. His concern has been for a ministry well equipped, alive, efficient, and devoted to its task. He represented the Council of Bishops on the Commission to Study the Episcopacy and the District Superintendency from 1972 to 1976 and worked closely with the companion Committee on the Ministry during the same years. The reports of both committees betray at important points the hallmarks of his influence.

In the Council of Bishops, Bishop Loder became in due time one of its most vocal members. He was another of the back row bishops, but he could move quickly into the aisle to participate in discussions. He had a keen sense of the possible implications of any course taken, and he was quick to point them out. He also had a propensity for making nominations. He probably exceeded most of his episcopal colleagues in the number of his nominations made and accepted. Bishop Loder was given many special assignments by the council. From 1974 to 1975 he served as its president. As a presiding officer, he had the ability to keep business moving rapidly, and he was often put in the chair of the General Conference when there was an unusually heavy amount of legislation to be considered.

The bishop also has an interest in the wider reaches of Methodism, and he was active in the World Methodist Council, where he was an officer for some years.

ROBERT F. LUNDY

Bishop Robert F. Lundy was elected by the 1964 Southeast Asia Central Conference. He was at the time a much trusted missionary in Malaya where he had served for some years. He favored the election of a national and did not want to be involved himself. But diverse national groups within the Southeast Asia Central Conference tended not to vote for each other, and twice before the problem had to be solved by turning to the election of a missionary. In 1964 none of the various nationals could receive a majority vote, and the conference turned to Dr. Lundy. After some persuasion he consented to the election.

Bishop Lundy's four-year episcopacy was a bridge episcopacy, which was what he wanted it to be. The next quadrennium the church became autonomous, and a national was elected.

Bishop Lundy returned to the States and served for a time in the Board of Missions. He then became executive secretary of the Southeastern Jurisdictional Council, following which he became pastor of Broad Street, Cleveland, Tennessee, in his native Holston Conference and later district superintendent of the Knoxville District.

EDWARD J. PENDERGRASS

Bishop Edward J. Pendergrass was elected by the 1964 Southeastern Jurisdictional Conference. He was at the time pastor of First Church, Orlando, Florida, the same pulpit from which his close friend Bishop John Branscomb had been elected twelve years before and from which Bishop Robert Blackburn would be elected eight years later. He had served all his ministry in the Florida Conference, as a pastor and as district superintendent. He was assigned to the Mississippi area, which he administered until his retirement in 1972.

Bishop Pendergrass has deep convictions to which he is forever loyal. He is a man of boldness and high courage, and he does not shrink from difficult decisions. His good judgment and fine balance help him take a practical approach to situations confronting him.

Bishop Pendergrass served Mississippi in some difficult days. When he arrived on the scene, he found a division of mind in both the Annual Conferences and many local churches. Ultra conservative individuals wanted to cling to the past, while many others felt the necessity for change had to be faced and change should be made. There had been a recent sad exodus of some promising more liberal young men of the conference to other parts of the country. Bishop Pendergrass felt that it was his responsibility to hold the church together and to be the bishop of all parties but at the same time to take a leadership role in harmony with his own convictions and the position of the larger church. He moved in on the situation with a firm sense of direction.

In his second quadrennium came the dissolution of the Central Jurisdiction, and he became bishop of four conferences in Mississippi, two black and two white. His leadership responsibility was to bring the four together into two conferences. The story of Bishop Pendergrass's faithfulness to this responsibility until he turned it over to Bishop Stokes in 1972 deserves to be remembered.

Bishop Pendergrass as a pastor and as a bishop was commited to evangelism and church growth. Wherever he went as a pastor, churches grew under his ministry even when they were located in unfavorable downtown situations. He was unapologetic for his emphasis upon church growth. He was concerned about numbers as long as numbers represented people. The steady continuing decline in membership in United Methodism since 1968 grieves his heart and sends him often to his knees.

Upon retirement Bishop and Mrs. Pendergrass moved back to their loved Florida to make their home in Lakeland, where the bishop accepted certain promotional responsibilities for Florida Southern College.

THOMAS M. PRYOR

Bishop Thomas M. Pryor was elected by the 1964 North Central Jurisdictional Conference. He was at the time pastor of First Church, Kalamazoo, Michigan, and had for some years been a leader in Michigan Methodism and pastor of some of its churches. He was assigned to the Chicago area, which he served until his retirement in 1972.

Bishop Pryor regretted that his active years in the episcopacy were limited to only eight. This feeling was aggravated by the fact that his birthday fell at a near point in the quadrennial calendar that cost him four more possible years of service.

Bishop Pryor belonged to the liberal school and did not hesitate to take advanced stands. He enthusiastically supported the ecumenical movement, the feminist movement, and movement to overcome racism and discrimination.

The bishop's pronounced interest in sociology led him to achieve a Ph.D. degree in that field. His appointment to the Chicago area gave him opportunity to make use of his sociological knowledge. The years that he was bishop in Chicago were particulaly difficult ones. Scores of his churches were in deteriorating communities where radical change in both constituency and program had to be worked through. It was a period of protest and confrontation which sometimes took violent form. He had to live with the slaying of at least one of his ministers who paid the last full measure of devotion for his loyalty to his desire to serve people. The bishop had to deal with both ultraradical and ultraconservative elements within the area. His lot was to be bishop in a day of tumult and in a center of that tumult, but he did not ask to be excused.

When Bishop Pryor retired, the council recognized his sociological interest by asking him to do a study of the urban church. He gave himself to this assignment with vigor for two years, amassing data, studying local situations, and enlisting the help of experts. The study came to a head at the meeting of the council at New Orleans in 1975 when a large portion of the time was devoted to its reception.

Bishop Pryor liked to visit Methodist fields around the world. During his retirement days he was the first of the bishops to visit China after it became open to visitors.

The bishop was regular in his attendance at council meetings but was never an officer, doubtless because his period as an active bishop was relatively short. He had a marked interest in worship, and the council called upon him to have charge of the celebration of the Communion at 1972 General Conference. He discharged this duty with skill and beauty.

Following retirement, Bishop and Mrs. Pryor made their winter home in Sarasota, Florida, and their summer home in Michigan. The bishop died suddenly in 1979.

The Episcopal Leadership Team 1940–1967

JOHN WESLEY SHUNGU

Bishop John Wesley Shungu was elected by the 1964 Africa Central Conference. He and Bishop Zunguze were the first native Africans to be elected by the Africa Central Conference. He had grown up in the Congo (now Zaire) and had served first as a school head and then as a pastor. He was assigned to the Zaire area, which he served until 1972.

Full of energy, Bishop Shungu was untiring in his willingness to meet the demands of the itinerate road. His name, John Wesley, fits him to perfection, for he is an ardent evangelist fully committed to the building of the church. His reports on his work were welcome features of the bishops' meetings which he attended.

In the Africa Central Conference term episcopacy prevails, and while he was reelected in 1968, he failed of reelection in 1972. He then returned to private life, entering business and taking up membership in a local church.

W. McFERRIN STOWE

Bishop W. McFerrin Stowe was elected by the 1964 South Central Jurisdictional Conference. He was at the time pastor of St. Luke's Church, Oklahoma City. Previously he had served pastorates in Oklahoma and Texas, and he had been for a period on the staff of the Board of Education in the Department of the Local Church. He was assigned to the Kansas area, which he served until 1972 when he was transferred to the Dallas-Fort Worth area. He served there until his retirement in 1980.

Bishop Stowe has a rich Methodist heritage on both sides of the family. In his veins flow some of the best blood of Methodism in Tennessee. His father, Dr. J. J. Stowe, was one of the most loved members of the Tennessee Conference and an able preacher and administrator. His mother was a McFerrin, a family that furnished a number of preachers for the church. One of them was the stalwart giant of a century ago, Dr. John B. McFerrin, who was the head of the Publishing House and had scarcely an equal in the M.E.

Church, South, in his day. Bishop Stowe appreciates this heritage and has sought to be true to it. His preaching and writings reflect his loyalty.

Bishop Stowe is a well-trained man. He has a Ph.D. degree, and he writes and preaches well. Several books and numerous articles have come from his pen. His sermons are well thought out, interest sustaining, and provocative. The bishops recognized his writing ability when they requested him to be the author of the Episcopal Address to the 1980 General Conference.

Upon retirement in 1980, Bishop and Mrs. Stowe continued to make their home in Dallas, where he became bishop in residence at Southern Methodist University.

R. MARVIN STUART

Bishop R. Marvin Stuart was elected by the 1964 Western Jurisdictional Conference from the pastorate of First Church, Palo Alto, California, where he had served for twelve years. He joined the North Indiana Conference originally but soom became one of "Bishop Baker's boys," the group of young preachers out of various seminaries whom Bishop Baker recruited in his attempt to build the church on the West Coast. Eight of these "boys" were elected to the episcopacy. Bishop Stuart was greatly attached to Bishop Baker, and when blindness had overtaken Bishop Baker, Bishop Stuart's son would read to him and write for him.

Bishop Stuart was also close to Bishop Tippett, who had been his bishop for sixteen years. It turned out that he in turn was to be Bishop Tippett's bishop for eight years as the latter had his retirement home in the area Bishop Stuart was administering. This closeness to Bishop Tippett continued after Bishop Stuart retired, and he gave devoted attention to Bishop Tippett in the days of his loss of Mrs. Tippett.

At the time of his election Bishop Stuart was assigned to the Denver area where he remained for eight years. During this time he was host to the 1971 meeting of the World Methodist Council. In 1972 he was transferred to the San Francisco area, which he served until retirement in 1980.

Bishop Stuart came from a conservative background,

reacted somewhat to it, and became a liberal, but he maintains respect for and tolerance of persons with less liberal viewpoints than his own. He was another of the bishops who usually sat on the back row, but he was less vocal than some of his companions. Yet he was a man of deep convictions, and he did not hesitate to speak up when he felt the need.

Bishop Stuart is a pastor by nature. During his days of serving a local congregation and exercising a strong pulpit ministry, he gave himself fully to a dedicated pastoral ministry. When he served an episcopal area, he kept the pastoral approach. From 1979 to 1980 he was the president of the Council of Bishops, and there he took the pastoral approach. He used ingenious methods in doing this and developed in the council a high degree of family consciousness. It was not surprising that upon his retirement the council asked him to be something of a pastor to the large number of retired bishops and their wives and the widows of deceased bishops, keeping in touch with them and alerting them to news related to the episcopal family. Mrs. Stuart was asked to join him in this pastoral arrangement.

Bishop Stuart was intent on developing a more effective ministry for the church. To this end he addressed himself to the problems of the parsonage family in retreats and fellowship experiences planned for ministers and their spouses in his area. In the Council of Bishops he was among these insisting that the council address itself to consideration of increasing family problems, both parsonage and lay families.

The bishop had a special interest in the training of district superintendents, and it was under his leadership that the present program of an annual training event for new district superintendents was developed.

Bishop Stuart retired in 1980, and he and Mrs. Stuart have made their home in Los Altos, California. He has assumed a position as director of a campaign to endow a chaplaincy at the University of the Pacific.

JAMES S. THOMAS

Bishop James S. Thomas was elected by the 1964 Central Jurisdictional Conference. He was a native of South Carolina and a son of the parsonage. His beginning pastoral ministry was spent in South Carolina, but most of his early years were in educational work. For some years he taught at Gammon Theological Seminary. At the time of his election he was serving on the staff of the Division of Higher Education of the General Board of Education, a position he occupied for eleven years. In this position he had important responsibilities, including counseling and offering guidance to black colleges of the church.

In 1964, anticipating the final dissolution of the Central Jurisdiction, that part of the Lexington Conference lying within the North Central Jurisdiction was merged with the geographical conferences with the consent of both the Central and the North Central Jurisdictions. Bishop Thomas was transferred with this fragment of the old Central Jurisdiction. A similar process was followed in the Northeastern Jurisdiction in the case of the old Washington and Delaware Conferences with Bishop Prince A. Taylor assigned to that jurisdiction. Bishop Thomas was assigned to the Des Moines area, which he served until 1976 when he was transferred to the East Ohio area.

Bishop Thomas has a composed appearance, but his sensitive nature sometimes causes him to suffer from inner tensions. He feels deeply all that he regards as wrong in the church, society, and the lives of individuals. His convictions run deep, and he can be firm when firmness is necessary.

Bishop Thomas is a scholarly man with a scholar's habits. He labors carefully over whatever he writes and weighs every word to be sure it is the exact word to use. In the council a paper prepared by his hand was backed by diligent research and long hours of laboring for perfection. He is theologically minded, and when he writes or preaches, it is from a strong theological perspective. He is by training and interest a man devoted to planning and execution, and in his area and in his larger church activities he gave large attention to program.

Bishop Thomas was the chairman of the commission which brought to the 1972 General Conference a revision of the Social Principles. At the time of union in 1968, both the Methodist Church and the Evangelical United Brethren

The Episcopal Leadership Team 1940-1967

Church had social statements in their *Disciplines*. The Methodist statement traced back to a Social Creed adopted by the 1908 General Conference of the Methodist Episcopal Church, by the 1914 General Conference of the Methodist Episcopal Church, South, by the 1916 General Conference of the Methodist Protestant Church, and by the Uniting Conference of 1938. The Evangelical United Brethren statement dated back to 1946. The statements of both churches were embodied in the 1968 *Discipline* of The United Methodist Church.

Successive General Conferences had amplified and added to the earlier statements of Social Principles by the various churches. The original Social Creed of 1908 was relatively brief and dealt primarily with economic issues.

It was evident in 1968 not only that some correlation of the two statements then embodied in the *Discipline* needed to be developed but also that new social issues needed to be addressed and some rethinking done upon approaches to older social issues. Accordingly a commission was appointed, and Bishop Thomas became the chairman. He gave to it skilled and dedicated leadership, and it was generally conceded that much of the credit for what was finally submitted to the 1972 General Conference belonged to him.

Bishop Thomas's responsibility as chairman involved no easy assignment. There was first of all a wide range of subjects to be handled. Dealing adequately with any one of them involved long hours of meticulous research, careful thought, and the expression in precise language of the position taken. Many issues to be considered were not a part of the social picture in an earlier era. Moreover, the statement being formulated was for a pluralistic church in which there would be persons for whom a reasoned case would have to be made for any position on almost any subject. The commission included persons from all sections of the country, whites and blacks, laymen and laywomen, pastors, district superintendents, university professors, and connectional persons who found themselves with pronounced differences of opinions at certain points.

Bishop Thomas, with his characteristic patience, his

deliberate movement, his quiet openness to all persons desiring to express a viewpoint, and his rare ability to bring matters to a conclusion, piloted the commission to the completion of its work, with only two dissenting votes. The new statement succinctly and clearly dealt with almost all the social problems touched upon in the two statements incorporated in the first *Discipline* of the new church as of 1968, and it dealt with some twenty social problems not touched upon in either previous statement. The new statement was adopted by the 1972 General Conference after extended debate but with modification at only a relatively few points.

Bishop Thomas was chosen to write the Episcopal Address to the 1976 General Conference at Portland, Oregon. He became president of the Council in 1984.

LANCE WEBB

Bishop Lance Webb was elected by the 1964 North Central Jurisdictional Conference from the pastorate of North Broadway Church, Columbus, Ohio. From this same church Bishop F. Gerald Ensley was elected to the episcopacy twelve years before. Previous to his pastorate at Columbus, Bishop Webb had been a pastor in Texas. He was one of the few bishops elected since Methodist union in 1939 who had served only one appointment in the jurisdiction in which he was elected. He was assigned to the Illinois area where he remained for twelve years. In 1976 he was assigned to the Iowa area where he served until retirement in 1980.

Bishop Webb is a hard working student. Gathering material and making copious notes are routine for him. He has an inquisitive mind, and he likes to ask questions. In the Council of Bishops and in other bodies he usually entered into the discussion, but it was normally by way of a provocative question rather than by way of an argument or a declaration. When he was asked to prepare a paper, he did it with carefulness. He has done a great deal of writing, and he has a large number of books to his credit. The year of his retirement saw the appearance of his religious novel, *Onesimus,* on which he had spent years of research and writing. Many bishops have written books, but few, if any, have attempted novel writing.

A major interest with Bishop Webb is worship, and he has made helpful contributions in this field. In 1964 he became chairman of the Commission of Worship, and he gave himself to this assignment with glad abandon. He also experimented personally with the development of worship materials. He is enamored with religious ceremony but insists that it be marked by good taste and meaningfulness. He tends to use high church dress and appurtenances that would have shocked the southern bishops who first knew him when he was a beginning preacher in Texas.

Another of Bishop Webb's interests is rural life and its relation to the church and the world. This was in order since his entire active episcopacy was spent in predominantly rural central Illinois, southern Illinois, and Iowa. He devoted attention to the rural church and sought to help lift the level of its performance in mission. He took leadership in a series of grain belt conferences designed to help rural society confront current problems and opportunities.

Bishop Webb retired in 1980, and he and Mrs. Webb moved to Pompano Beach, Florida. The bishop has continued his writing and frequently travels throughout the country lecturing and preaching, largely under the auspices of the Upper Room. Later the Webbs moved to Dallas, Texas.

ESCRIVAO A. ZUNGUZE

Bishop Escrivao A. Zunguze was elected in his absence by the 1964 Africa Central Conference. From a family of African royal blood he had been a pastor in Mozambique. For four years he was a missionary to his own people, working in the gold mines in South Africa. He was for a time administrative assistant to Bishop Ralph Dodge when Bishop Dodge could not get into Mozambique. Upon election he was assigned to the Mozambique area, which he served until his retirement in 1976. His successor, Bishop Almeida Penicela, was seriously injured in an automobile accident shortly after his election, and Bishop Zunguze again took over the area until Bishop Penicela could resume his responsibilities.

Bishop Zunguze was an unusually able and forceful preacher and a good singer. He attented the meetings of the

Council of Bishops on an average of about once a year. He watched with interest the various concerns to which the council addressed itself, so many of which were essentially American in character. He did not speak except to report on his work.

Upon his retirement in 1976 Bishop Zunguze continued to live in Cambine where he taught in a Bible School until his death in October, 1980.

ALFRED J. SHAW

Bishop Alfred J. Shaw was elected by the 1965 Central Conference of Southern Asia. At the time he was secretary of Christian education for the Central Conference. Much of his ministry was spent in educational work. For a considerable period he was an instructor in Lucknow Christian College. For three years he served as pastor of Central Church, Lucknow, and at the same time as district superintendent. At one time he was editor of *The Indian Christian Witness,* and he continued to write often for the paper after his days as editor were over. He came from a long line of preachers and was himself a third generation minister. From 1948 to 1949 he was a Crusade Scholar at Syracuse University. Upon election he was assigned to the Bombay area, which he served for four years. After that he served the Delhi area for four years, and he retired in 1972.

Bishop Shaw was adept at administration. He attended the Council of Bishops with interest but generally had little to say unless called upon. Perhaps this was because he felt that so many of the matters largely represented American church affairs. In meetings in India, however, he was a ready participant in discussions, and he often took a leading role.

The families of Bishop Singh and Bishop Shaw were closely connected; the daughter of Bishop Singh married a son of Bishop Shaw.

Upon retirement Bishop Shaw made his home in Bareilly, India. For a time he was called out of retirement to serve the Bombay area following the death of Bishop Joshi, until the Central Conference could elect another bishop.

The last time the Council of Bishops saw Bishop Shaw was at the 1980 General Conference in Indianapolis. He died suddenly at his home in Bareilly in January, 1981. At the time of his death he was just finishing a book, *Christianity and Social Change in India.*

FRANZ SCHAFER

Bishop Franz Schafer was elected by the 1966 General Conference of Southern Europe following the death of Bishop Ferdinand Sigg. He was a district superintendent in the Switzerland Annual Conference at the time. He was the second Swiss to be elected a Methodist bishop; the other was his predecessor, Bishop Sigg. Bishop Schafer was first elected for a four-year term. In 1970 he was reelected, and in 1974 he was reelected for life.

Bishop Schafer has had to administer perhaps the most unusual area in Methodism in its composition since conferences are on both sides of the iron curtain. His area has included Switzerland and Austria on one side of the curtain, and Poland, Czechoslovakia, Hungary, Yugoslavia, and Bulgaria on the other. He also has had the work in North Africa. Most of the bishop's conferences are small and represent in some cases only fragments of what were once mission fields of a Methodism that prior to World War II boasted of being a world church.

Bishop Schafer has been unable to get into some of the countries beyond the iron curtain, and his administration has had to be by remote control there. The variety of languages used has complicated for him both presiding and corresponding. The weakness of the church in many places in size of membership and in resources has presented almost insoluble problems for him, as have the legal requirements on the church obtaining in several countries of the area. The vastness of the area has necessitated an unusual amount of travel often made under severe restrictions.

Bishop Schafer has spoken infrequently in the Council of Bishops. He seems totally unaware of the fact that most bishops speak only one language, while he can speak three. He is unassuming almost to a fault. He is content to live simply, and he asks for little.

There is in the bishop the same pietistic and personal religious emphasis that has been traditionally strong in German and Swiss Methodism. He is a man of faith and prayer who seeks to lead others to the Savior. He has a social conscience, and like European Methodism with its traditional emphasis upon social service, he believes that faith should manifest itself in active good will.

L. SCOTT ALLEN

Bishop L. Scott Allen was elected by a special session of the Central Jurisdictional Conference called in 1967 to replace Bishop M. Lafayette Harris, who had died. He was the last bishop to be elected by the Central Jurisdiction, fourteen in all, beginning with the election of Bishops W. A. C. Hughes and Lorenzo H. King in 1940. At the time of his election he was the editor of the *Central Christian Advocate*. It was from this same position that Bishops R. E. Jones, Alexander P. Shaw, Robert N. Brooks, and Prince A. Taylor, Jr., had been elected before him.

Before his editorship he had served pastorates and had taught at Clark College. He was consecrated at McKendree Church, Nashville, the mother church of the Tennessee Conference of the Southeastern Jurisdiction. He was assigned to the Gulf Coast area, which included the black conferences in Alabama, Mississippi, and Florida. When the Central Jurisdiction was dissolved in 1968, he was assigned to the Southeastern Jurisdiction. There he was assigned to the newly created Holston area with residence at Knoxville, Tennessee. After serving eight years in the Holston area, he was transferred to the Charlotte area, which he began to serve in 1976.

The bishop is a fair man. In council meetings his approach was not to ask what was politically possible, but what was fair and right. Once he reached a conclusion, he tended to stand by it somewhat rigidly, but he would change course if honestly persuaded.

Bishop Allen has been a staunch defender of the rights of his people. In taking his stand for such rights he will not allow himself to become ill-spirited, but in a matter-of-fact, steady way will appeal to what is proper and Christian. In dealing with his own people he counsels that they themselves be a part of the solution of the problems with which they are beset. He is interested in ways to strengthen the black local church, especially through an adequately trained and consecrated ministry.

Bishop Allen is a powerful preacher, who can deeply move audiences. His preaching is scriptural, thought provoking, and fervent and speaks to both the head and the heart. The bishop has a good voice, and he often breaks into a song at the end of a sermon. Presiding in an Annual Conference, he would sometimes start a song, never failing to get the right pitch.

Bishop Allen belongs in the category of the church lawyer. His peers generally recognized that no one knew the *Discipline* better than he did. He came to every council meeting with his *Discipline* and the decisions of the Judicial Council. When finally in 1980 the General Conference saw fit to put a bishop upon the Committee on Correlation responsible for the finalizing of the text of the *Discipline,* Bishop Allen was chosen for the assignment.

The bishop is also a student of parliamentary law. Robert's *Rules of Order* is another book he has sought to master. He is a good presiding officer, and he was often chosen for the chair when there promised to be some possibility of a parliamentary tangle. Once he arrived at a parliamentary conclusion, he held firmly to his position. On one or two occasions when there was an appeal from one of his decisions, the house overruled him, but generally his decisions were so respected that they stood without appeal.

Bishop Allen ranked high in the regard of the Council of Bishops, and it gave him numerous important and sometimes difficult assignments. In his own College of Bishops in the Southeastern Jurisdiction he was greatly loved and respected and was one of the favorites of the group.

He has been a natural leader of the black membership resident within the geographical bounds of the Southeastern Jurisdiction, and when the merger of the jurisdictions came in 1968, his sense of justice, his wisdom, and his reasonableness contributed in a large way to its successful accomplishment.

V
EPISCOPAL LEADERSHIP IN A CRITICAL ERA

Reference is in order to the leadership role played by the episcopacy in the critical era in the life of the world and the church represented by the sixties.

The bishops elected in 1948, 1952, 1956, 1960, and 1964 in particular found themselves called to spend their active episcopacy during one of the most turbulent times in recent history. It was a violent time of rioting and burning in many cities and of sometimes taking the law into one's hands. It was also a time of frequent nonviolent but dramatic and forceful demonstrations of protest. Behind these lay the agelong frustrations of the poor, the exploited, and the disenfranchised who decided that the time had come to voice their demands for full rights.

Also behind many protests lay the reactions of young people to the Korean and Vietnam wars, and to the inequities and repression they regarded as being imposed by the power structure. Few college campuses were free of demonstrations of some kind, and few cities did not see youth take to the streets in protest.

In the same period many women orgainzed to demand rights that womanhood had not enjoyed before and to press for due recognition.

A number of minorities, not too visible before, also began to take up the pattern of protest and to make common cause of their concerns.

Demonstrations took such varied forms as staging sit-ins, blocking traffic, occupying offices, and disrupting assemblies. The bishops discovered that even General Conferences and meetings of the council could not expect to be exempt from disruption during this period. Every active bishop had to live with the effects of the turbulence of these days upon the people of his area, many of whom were directly involved in them, and upon the life of the churches. Bishops whose areas included large metropolitan centers found their administrative tasks sometimes quite taxing.

During this same period the Methodist Church in the United States found itself confronted directly and dramatically with problems related to race. It had developed for more than a century and a half as a church possessed of a larger minority membership than any other Protestant church. Included in its membership in the United States were blacks, Hispanics, and Native Americans in sufficient numbers to be organized into Annual Conferences, as well as a considerable number of Orientals who had once been organized into separate Annual Conferences but by now had been absorbed into the surrounding geographic conferences. In addition, the Methodist Church included conferences overseas from the United States, scattered throughout half a hundred countries representing all races and many difficult cultures. The Evangelical United Brethren Church also had overseas conferences as well as connections with a number of united churches.

A church so diverse in character could not face the racial problems of such a time from the position of a concerned outsider passively looking on, which was what the mostly white denominations could do. Rather, Methodists had to face the racial situation as a family in which all members were involved. The story of the part the episcopacy of Methodism played in this situation is yet to be told fully.

One may well begin to look at the story by examining the Supreme Court decision of 1954 which outlawed segregation in the public schools. Some persons in the South anticipated the decision and sought to prepare people to accept it for the move toward justice and freedom for all children that it represented. In the Nashville region several months before the decision was announced, under the leadership of Dr. John Q. Schisler of the General Board of Education of the Methodist Church and with the cooperation of the resident

145

bishop, a three-day conference of Methodist leaders was called at a state park to consider how the church could be most helpful when the decision finally came.

In the period immediately following the decision, a group of southern church leaders and educational leaders was called together by Dr. William M. Elliott, then moderator of the Presbyterian Church, U. S. The group included top officials of the Presbyterian, Episcopal, Disciples, Southern Baptist, and Methodist churches and leading educators from some large southern cities. The purpose of the group was to help pave the way in the South for cooperation in the implementation of the decision. The group met several times over a period of two years and was funded by the generosity of a major foundation. It sought to do its work quietly and informally. What the final result of its efforts may have been remains unknown. Bishops John W. Branscomb and Roy H. Short represented the Southeastern College of Bishops in this group.

Doubtless many other efforts seeking to win acceptance and implementation of the decision could be pointed out, were the facts fully known.

While individual Methodist bishops sought locally to make what contributions they might to the acceptance of the decision, the council as a whole gave strong formal endorsement to it.

The decade of the sixties witnessed an increasing demand by the black population of the country for access to public accommodations, freedom to participate at all levels of society as first-class citizens, and the enjoyment of the right accorded to every American under the Constitution. The demand was dramatized in various ways, such as demonstration marches; the most significant one was a march on Washington in August, 1968, by 200,000 persons both black and white to demand equal rights for black citizens.

Some persons resisted the movement, and others feared it. Generally the bishops of Methodism endorsed the movement, and some of them participated in the demonstrations. The bishops saw a sign of hope in Dr. Martin Luther King with his prophetic leadership, his refusal to be daunted, and his adherence to the strategy of nonviolence. Some bishops, particularly in the South, had to find ways to help some members of their congregations to adjust to the new situation and to see that full liberty for all persons is not only American but also Christian.

One incident during this period which merits a review of episcopal participation was the long-to-be-remembered march from Selma to Montgomery, Alabama, March 21–25, 1965. The march started with 3,200, but its ranks were swelled finally to 25,000. The march was guarded by 4,000 troops dispatched by President Johnson. Bishops John Wesley Lord, Charles F. Golden, and Richard C. Raines were among those who joined the march.

The Supreme Court decision on segregation in the public schools and the civil rights movement had decided overtones. The Methodist Church had segregation built into its structure, with separate black conferences in the Methodist Episcopal Church since 1864 and black conferences set apart in a separate jurisdiction since Methodist union in 1939. The temper of the times challenged Methodism to set its own house in order.

The Episcopal Address of 1956, written by Bishop Fred P. Corson, squarely addressed the issue, declaring that there was no place in the Methodist Church for segregation. This meant that every local church should be open to all persons regardless of race. Hundreds of Methodist local churches by choice were confined to white members, while many hundreds more were confined to white membership not because they wanted to exclude blacks but simply because blacks did not choose to attend or no effort was made to reach them. Hundreds of black churches, while not deliberately excluding whites from attendance or membership, did not seek them.

The 1963 Council of Bishops issued a statement on race, affirming the right of all persons of all races to membership in and the privilege of worship in all our churches. This position met with little adverse reaction generally but was heavily resisted at some points. A dramatic incident occurred when Bishops Charles F. Golden and James K. Mathews attempted to attend church services together at Galloway Memorial Church in Jackson, Mississippi, and were turned away.

The day soon came, however, when with reasonably slight resistance the average Methodist congregation became open to all persons regardless of race. Once the principle of the fully open church was established, relatively few blacks chose to identify with a predominantly white congregation or vice versa. Although liberals who fought for the desegregation of the local churches saw the coming of the open church as the fulfillment of an ideal, the black constituency of the church had its proper cautions.

Black local churches were no more anxious to lose their identity than white churches. Moreover, the black worship experience had its own particular appeal and value. And beyond that, the black local church played a role in black life that could not be surrendered without irreparable loss. Many blacks did not want to find themselves a minority in a predominantly white local congregation. The bishops therefore encouraged fully open local churches, but at the same time they recognized the importance of the predominantly black local church, as well as that of other ethnic minority congregations. The melting pot theory, which Methodism had followed for some years, gave way to a new appreciation of ethnic identity and, twenty years after the battle for open local churches, to a major churchwide quadrennial emphasis upon the ethnic minority church.

Another area in Methodism that involved segregation in its corporate life was the Central Jurisdiction. The establishment of the Central Jurisdiction in 1939 had been one of the devices by which union had been achieved. It represented, however, the addition of a black power unit, for the Methodist Episcopal Church already had separate black churches and Annual Conferences and black bishops elected upon separate ballots. In fact, some black leaders objected to its creation but went along in the interest of union, although they hoped it would not be a permanent feature of the church.

For a dozen years or so, all went fairly smoothly. The Central Jurisdiction elected some dynamic persons to the episcopacy, and because of the guarantees to each jurisdiction of a given number of board members, the black constituency found itself with larger participation in the board life of the church than ever before. White and black bishops serving in overlapping territory sometimes found ways to work together. But by the sixties bishops, and much of the church, recognized that a jurisdiction based upon race ought not be continued with the church's endorsement.

In January, 1958, a called session of the Council of Bishops was held in Ocean City, New Jersey, for the sole purpose of considering the situation. Each bishop was asked to state freely his thinking for the benefit of the twelve bishops who were on the Committee on the Jurisdictional System created by the previous General Conference. A few bishops entertained fears of the possible reaction in their areas to the abolition of the jurisdiction, but the majority of the bishops agreed that the abolition was nevertheless something to which the church must address itself. Bishop Willis King, in the name of the Central Jurisdiction bishops, submitted a paper stating that they favored the elimination of the jurisdiction when both groups were ready for action.

The twelve bishops on the Committee on the Jurisdictional System were all active participants. The first result of the work of the committee and the subsequent General Conference action was provision for legislation which made crossovers of jurisdictional lines possible for churches or conferences. This legislation was utilized in only a few cases.

By the midsixties it was apparent that something more needed to be done. On every hand there was mounting dissatisfaction with the existence in the church of a racially structured jurisdiction. Each session of the council saw the matter come up in one form or another. At a meeting in Houston, Texas, in 1965 following a paper by Bishop Prince Albert Taylor entitled "Race in the Methodist Church" and one by the writer, "The Pastoral Role of the Episcopacy in the Racial Situation," on motion of Bishop Vernon Middleton a committee was appointed to work out plans for a truly inclusive church. The bishops' Committee on Race, thus ordered, was composed of Bishops Wicke, Raines, Golden, Stuart, and Short. The committee began its work the following summer and continued to operate throughout the remainder of the quadrennium. The final elimination of the

Central Jurisdiction came with the adoption of Evangelical United Brethren-Methodist union in 1968; the Constitution of the new church omitted provision for such a jurisdiction.

The Northeastern and North Central Jurisdictional Conferences anticipated the final dissolution of the Central Jurisdiction by four years. In 1964 the Lexington Conference was dissolved, and that portion of it falling within the North Central Jurisdiction was absorbed. Bishop James S. Thomas, elected by the 1964 Central Jurisdictional Conference, became a bishop of the North Central Jurisdiction and was assigned to the Iowa area. Similarly, in 1964 the Washington and Delaware Conferences went into the Northeastern Jurisdiction, and Bishop Prince Albert Taylor, Jr., elected by the Central Jurisdiction in 1956, was assigned to the newly created New Jersey area.

In October, 1966, the Southeastern Jurisdictional Council met in Jackson, Mississippi. On the opening evening Bishop Short brought a paper based upon the text "Ye can discern the face of the sky, but can ye not discern the signs of the times?" It was a plea for the Southeastern Jurisdiction to face realistically the matter of racial structures in Methodism. The message hit the front page of the Jackson papers the next morning, but for some reason it was not reported in the general Methodist press.

This opening evening set the tone of the entire meeting, and while the Jurisdictional Council had no power to act for the Jurisdictional Conference or the Annual Conferences, the prevailing judgment of the group was that the day had come when the church should eliminate racial structures as quickly as possible. The bishops were particularly encouraged by the response of so many lay persons in the group as well as by so many ministers. The Jackson meeting undoubtedly went far to pave the way in the Southeast for the final elimination of such structures beginning in 1968.

In 1968 with the dissolution of the Central Jurisdiction and the allocation of the remaining conferences to the South Central and Southeastern Jurisdictions, Bishop Charles F. Golden was assigned to the Western Jurisdiction where he was appointed to the San Francisco area; Bishop Noah W. Moore,

Jr., to the South Central Jurisdiction where he was assigned to the Nebraska area; and Bishop L. Scott Allen to the Southeastern Jurisdiction where he was assigned to the Holston area.

The year 1968 saw the beginning of conference merger in the South Central and Southeastern Jurisdictions. In some sections the merger process presented more problems to be worked out than in others.

One such matter included the assurance that the black ministry and membership as a minority in the merged conferences would be granted fair recognition in the cabinet and in the composition and plans of conference boards and agencies.

Bishop Aubrey G. Wilson deserves special mention for his dedication to working out merger in Louisiana, a task to which he untiringly gave himself. Bishop Paul Hardin gave creative leadership to merger in South Carolina, and the process begun so effectively under him was carried to completion by Bishop Edward L. Tullis, Bishop Hardin's successor. Bishop Edward J. Pendergrass faced with courage and positiveness the working out of merger in Mississippi, and his example was followed by his successor Bishop Mack Stokes. Bishop W. Kenneth Goodson in Alabama, Bishop J. O. Smith in Georgia, and Bishop H. Ellis Finger in the Nashville area gave similar leadership.

The focal points of the Central Jurisdiction in 1968 were the cities of New Orleans, Atlanta, and Nashville and the states of South Carolina and Mississippi where the largest concentration of black membership was to be found. At these points skill was needed to accomplish the kind of merger that would stand the test of rightness and of effectiveness. In the Texas, Missouri, Arkansas, Virginia, North Carolina, Holston, Florida, and Kentucky Conferences, merger was accomplished with relative dispatch.

The first former Central Jurisdiction member to be appointed a district superintendent in a merged conference in the South was Dr. J. C. Peters, appointed by Bishop Earl G. Hunt, Jr., to the Winston-Salem District of the Western North

Carolina Conference. Since then, many blacks have been named as district superintendents in merged conferences.

Appointments of black pastors to predominantly white churches and of white pastors to predominantly black churches have not been too numerous to date. Bishop John Wesley Lord appointed Dr. Edward Carroll to a predominantly white church, Marvin Memorial, Baltimore, from which he was elected to the episcopacy. In 1961 Bishop Scott Allen appointed Dr. H. Walter Willis, a black, to Kern Memorial, Oak Ridge, Tennessee, also a predominantly white congregation. The bishops of the church are committed to open itinerancy but practical application of this commitment is at this time moving only slowly.

The years since the abolition of the Central Jurisdiction have seen the election of black bishops in every jurisdiction: Bishops Roy C. Nichols, Edward G. Carroll, and F. Herbert Skeete in the Northeastern; Bishop Edsel A. Ammons in the North Central; Bishops Ernest T. Dixon, Jr., and William T. Handy, Jr., in the South Central; Bishop Melvin G. Talbert in the Western; and Bishop Ernest H. Newman in the Southeastern. The same years have seen Bishops Prince Albert Taylor, Charles Golden, and Roy Nichols serve as president of the Council of Bishops, and Bishop James Thomas elected to prepare the Episcopal Address in 1976.

VI
NEW LEADERSHIP FOR A NEW CHURCH

Union between the Evangelical United Brethren Church and the Methodist Church was consummated at a Uniting Conference held in Dallas, Texas, in 1968. The story of the union is told fully by Bishop Paul Washburn in his book, *An Unfinished Church*.

The Plan of Union provided that all bishops, active and retired, of the two uniting churches would be bishops in the new church. Certificates indicating membership in the Council of Bishops of the new church, signed by the president and secretary of the Board of Bishops of the Evangelical United Brethren Church and the president and secretary of the Council of Bishops of the Methodist Church, were given to all bishops.

At the time of union in 1968 nine bishops of the Board of Bishops of the former Evangelical United Brethren Church became a part of the Council of Bishops of The United Methodist Church. Bishop George E. Epp, retired, had been a bishop for thirty-eight years; Bishops Reuben H. Mueller and Harold R. Heininger for fourteen years; Bishop J. Gordon Howard for eleven years; Bishops H. W. Kaebnick, W. Maynard Sparks, and Paul M. Herrick for ten years, Bishop Paul W. Milhouse for eight years; and Bishop Paul A. Washburn had just been elected. Bishops Epp, Herrick, and Howard all died in the early years of the united church and sketches of them appear in *Nineteen Bishops* by Bishop Milhouse and in the *History of the Council of Bishops* by this author.

153

THE EPISCOPAL LEADERSHIP ROLE IN UNITED METHODISM
REUBEN H. MUELLER

Bishop Reuben H. Mueller was elected by the 1954 General Conference of the Evangelical United Brethren Church. At that time he was the general secretary of Christian education. Bishop Mueller was originally a minister in the Evangelical Church prior to the union of the United Brethren and the Evangelical Churches in 1946. His assignment following his election was to the North Central area. Upon merger of the Evangelical United Brethren Church and the Methodist Church in 1968, he was assigned to the Indianapolis area, which he served until his retirement in 1972.

The bishop was a master administrator. For some years before union in 1968 the bishops of his church as a group looked to him as a leader. Bishop Mueller more than anyone else led the Evangelical United Brethren Church into union. He felt strongly that union ought to be accomplished, and he worked with diligence and skill toward that end. The Plan of Union at many points reflected his wisdom and concerns. He was devotedly loyal to the tradition out of which he came, and he was anxious to see the best in that tradition continued in the new church.

Bishop Mueller was quite naturally the first of the bishops coming out of the Evangelical United Brethren tradition to serve as the president of the Council of Bishops. He held this office from 1969 to 1970.

Bishop Mueller continued throughout his life his interest in Christian education, which had early spotted him for church-wide leadership. He was a powerful leader of the World Council of Christian Education and was its president for a number of years.

Another of the bishop's interests was in ecumenical affairs. From 1963 to 1966 he was the president of the National Council of Churches. These were years of stress that brought many problems for this council, and the bishop's firm, courageous, fair leadership proved to be one of the council's strongest assets during this time. The bishop was active in the World Council of Churches and was a member of its central committee for some years.

Upon retirement Bishop Mueller first made his home at Naperville, Illinois, and then at Franklin, Indiana, where he died in July, 1982.

HAROLD R. HEININGER

Bishop Harold R. Heininger was elected by the 1954 General Conference of the Evangelical United Brethren Church. He came out of the Evangelical Association constituency of that church. At the time of his election he was president of Evangelical Theological Seminary, a post he had held for fourteen years. He had been a faculty member since 1923. He was assigned to the Northwestern area.

At the time of union in 1968, all seven Evangelical United Brethren bishops were eligible to continue for one more quadrennium, regardless of age. Thus Bishop Heininger could have remained, and the Minnesota area with which much of his area was to be merged was wide open after the retirement of Bishop Nall, who had been serving the Minnesota area of the Methodist Church. However, Bishop Heininger chose to retire. He felt that he had reached a time when he no longer needed heavy responsibility, and he wanted the way opened for the last General Conference of the Evangelical United Brethren Church to elect a bishop. The 1968 General Conference elected Dr. Paul Washburn, who at the next session of the North Central Jurisdictional Conference was assigned to the Minnesota area.

The bishop's conversation and sermons were salted with wit and pleasantries. He knew the art of finding human, pertinent, and oftentimes humorous illustrations that added to the popularity of his preaching. He loved to sing, especially the great hymns of the faith. Even in his later years he was an enthusiastic member of the choir at the retirement home where he lived.

The bishop was a careful and conscientious student. For many years he taught theology, and his theological interest continued throughout his life. He was fully familiar with the various schools of theological thought, and amidst the clash of so many theological voices he was well able to maintain a reason for the faith that was in him.

Bishop Heininger had a concern for missions, and for some

years prior to union he was the president of the Board of Missions of the Evangelical United Brethren Church. In the years immediately preceding the 1968 merger he gave significant leadership to working out the problems relating to the consolidating of the work of the two churches overseas from the United States.

Bishop Heininger was a thoughtful and considerate person. He was forever trying to do something for others. In his retirement he sent letters of cheer and encouragement to friends everywhere.

Upon retirement Bishop and Mrs. Heininger moved to Naperville, and a few years later to a United Methodist home at Lebanon, Ohio. Bishop Heininger died in 1983. Bishop Clymer began the tribute to him at the Council Memorial Service with the words "Harold Heininger was no ordinary man."

HERMAN W. KAEBNICK

Bishop Herman W. Kaebnick was elected by the 1958 General Conference of the Evangelical United Brethren Church. He had been executive secretary of the General Council on Administration and before that a pastor and conference superintendent in Pennsylvania. He was assigned to the Eastern Episcopal area, with headquarters in Harrisburg. In 1968 he was assigned to the Harrisburg area of the new United Methodist Church, which meant that he continued to serve the same churches that he had been serving plus the Methodist churches who had lost their episcopal leader, Bishop Booth, by death only shortly before union. Bishop Kaebnick served this area until his retirement in 1972.

Bishop Kaebnick carried himself with the erectness of a soldier. He had a rich singing voice and in his young manhood had received vocal training. The soul of courtesy and kindness, he could express himself beautifully and in well-chosen words. A letter from him to a friend was often one to be treasured for the warmth of its expression and its rare flow of words.

Following his retirement Bishop Kaebnick did not attend again either the meetings of the council or the General

Conference. This absence was due in part to health reasons, but it was due also to his frugality and unwillingness to spend the church's money for himself. Since retirement he has made his home in Hershey, Pennsylvania.

W. MAYNARD SPARKS

Bishop W. Maynard Sparks was elected by the 1958 General Conference of the Evangelical United Brethren Church. He was the youngest of the bishops elected that year. At the time he was chaplain and teacher at Lebanon Valley College. Previously he had held pastorates in western Pennsylvania.

He was assigned to the work on the West Coast, where he served with devotion. As Evangelical United Brethren–Methodist union got under way, he found his task far from an easy one since several focal points of opposition to the union were in his conferences, especially in the Northwest and Canada.

With the coming of union in 1968 Bishop Sparks was assigned to the Seattle area. With the death of Bishop Palmer in 1971, he was given also the Portland area including the work in Alaska. He carried this heavy double responsibility until his retirement in 1972.

One of the chief characteristics of the bishop is his genuine brotherliness. He possesses tenderness and understanding that make him rejoice with those who rejoice and weep with those who weep. He knows personally what it is to "walk a mile with sorrow," but his faith has sustained and kept him and made him all the more an effective minister.

Bishop Sparks has been a warm-hearted, evangelical preacher, and his messages have inspired and blessed his hearers. He has proclaimed a full-rounded gospel that claimed every area of life for his Lord.

Upon retirement the bishop has continued to make his home in Sacramento, California, where his first episcopal headquarters had been.

PAUL W. MILHOUSE

Bishop Paul W. Milhouse was elected a bishop of the Evangelical United Brethren Church in 1960 by mail ballot following the sudden death of Bishop Lyle L. Baughman.

Election by mail ballot was a procedure allowed in the Evangelical United Brethren Church in case of a vacancy in the episcopal panel. Bishop Milhouse has the distinction of being the only bishop of the United Methodist Church elected in this manner. That Bishop Milhouse was thus elected speaks of how widely he was known and how highly he was regarded throughout the Evangelical United Brethren Church. The Southwestern area became his episcopal assignment with residence at Kansas City. He was the executive secretary of the Council on Administration at the time of his election. Previously he had served as an editor of church publications and in the pastorate in the Illinois Conference. With Evangelical United Brethren Methodist union in 1968, he was assigned to the Oklahoma area, which he served until retirement in 1980.

Bishop Milhouse believes the episcopal office was but one more servant responsibility laid upon him by the church. He has a keen, observant mind and studious habits. Whenever he was asked to present a paper by the Council of Bishops, his paper would be a systematic marshaling of facts and arguments. He has maintained throughout his life his writing habits, developed first as a schoolboy when he wrote a weekly column for his hometown paper in Illinois, and he has authored thirteen books. Probably the book for which he will be longest remembered is his story of the bishops of the Evangelical United Brethren Church from 1941 to 1968.

Bishop Milhouse has always been committed to the gospel of hard work. He studied hard. He labored consistently at his assigned task, and he traveled tirelessly the Southwestern area of the Evangelical United Brethren Church, which included Iowa, Kansas, Missouri, Nebraska, Oklahoma, and Texas. And he did the same thing when his assignment was the Oklahoma area of The United Methodist Church. He worked hard at planning and promoting the program of his episcopal areas, and he was by nature and previous experience a master of this. He had a green thumb and found relaxation from his episcopal task by occasional yard work.

During his twelve years on the Oklahoma area, Bishop

Milhouse had the responsibility for the Indian Mission. He thus became more knowlegeable of this important minority in United Methodism than any of his contemporaries in the council.

The Council of Bishops has great respect for Bishop Milhouse. It knows him as a bishop of solid convictions, with a fine sense of balance and a rich store of practical wisdom. He is recognized as being democratic in spirit and capable of being firm when firmness is necessary. The Council called upon the bishop for many important assignments and chose him as its president in 1977.

Upon retirement in 1980, Bishop and Mrs. Milhouse continued to make their home in Oklahoma City, and the bishop accepted a connection with Oklahoma City University.

PAUL A. WASHBURN

Bishop Paul A. Washburn was elected by the 1968 General Conference of the Evangelical United Brethren Church meeting in Dallas, Texas, which was that church's last General Conference. In its closing hours Bishop Washburn was elected and installed. He thus became the last of the long line of bishops running back to Otterbein and Albright. In the consecration of Asbury in 1784, Philip William Otterbein, a United Brethren minister, participated. Parelleling this, Bishop Reuben H. Meuller, who was presiding, decided to ask a Methodist bishop to participate in the installation of the last bishop elected in the Evangelical United Brethren Church, and he chose Bishop Roy H. Short for this honor.

Bishop Washburn had been for some years a pastor in the Illinois Conference. As the process of union with the Methodist Church got under way, he was asked to give full time to the work of the Commission on Union, and of all the members of the commission, both Evangelical United Brethren and Methodist, none gave himself or herself more completely to the details of perfecting legislation and the demands of voluminous correspondence and travel than Bishop Washburn. In the Commission on Union he took a strong position that what was involved was not merger but union, and that what was to be sought was a genuinely new, united church. At the Uniting Conference Bishop Washburn was assigned to the North Central Jurisdiction, and at that jurisdiction's conference he was assigned to the Minnesota area, which he served for four years. In 1972 he was assigned to the Chicago area, which he administered until his retirement in 1980.

Bishop Washburn is a hard-working, scholarly type of individual. His labors in the perfection of the starting legislation of The United Methodist Church leave the church forever in debt to him. In the Council of Bishops, Bishop Washburn was often asked to prepare a working paper to set the stage for some council discussion, and these papers exhibited the careful research and penetrating thought so characteristic of him.

The bishop was often called upon for special service during the first eight years after union, when someone was needed who could bring to bear the contribution of the Evangelical United Brethren tradition. From 1972 to 1976 he was president of the Board of Global Ministries.

Upon retirement in 1980, Bishop and Mrs. Washburn continued to make their home at Wheaton, Illinois. At the request of the Council of Bishops he has written a history of Evangelical United Brethren-Methodist union, *An Unfinished Church*.

A. JAMES ARMSTRONG

A. James Armstrong was elected bishop by the 1968 North Central Jurisdictional Conference. At the time he was the pastor of Broadway Church, Indianapolis, and before that he had been a pastor in the Florida Conference. He was a son of the parsonage, but his father died when Bishop Armstrong was quite young. He entered the conference at a youthful age and took his seminary work after he had served several pastorates. One of the inimitable characters of Florida Methodism, Dr. P. M. Boyd of First Church, Jacksonville, and friends in that church helped Bishop Armstrong go to seminary after he already had heavy family responsibilities. The bishop was only forty-three at the time of his election and thus became one of the rather small group of bishops of the Methodist Church in the United States to be elected in their forties.

Bishop Armstrong was assigned to the Dakotas area, which continued as his assignment for twelve years. In 1980 he was assigned to the Indiana area from which he was elected.

He resigned from the episcopacy in 1983.

WILLIAM R. CANNON

Bishop William R. Cannon was elected by the 1968 Southeastern Jurisdictional Conference. At the time he was dean of the Candler School of Theology, where he had been a member of the faculty for twenty-four years. His only experience as a pastor came at the beginning of his ministry when he served for one year the college church at Old Emory at Oxford and for a brief period a smaller church in Atlanta. He was the first bachelor to be elected to the episcopacy in the Methodist Church since the election of Bishop McKendree in 1808. He was assigned to the Raleigh area, which he served for four years. For a portion of this time he took over the Virginia area when Bishop Herrick was forced to retire because of his failing health. In 1972 Bishop Cannon was assigned to the Atlanta area, where he remained for eight years. In 1980 he was returned to the Raleigh area for the final quadrennium of his active episcopacy.

The bishop is indeed a character. He is warm, outgoing, and delightfully human. His emotions run deep, and he does not hesitate to express them by a warm embrace. A beautiful example of this came in 1964 at the Southeastern Jurisdictional Conference when four bishops were elected. In the voting for the fourth bishop the two persons getting the highest votes were Dr. Cannon and Dr. Earl Hunt of the Holston Conference. Dr. Hunt had been Dr. Cannon's pupil at Emory, and they were warm friends. When the chair announced the election of Dr. Hunt, Dr. Cannon literally ran across the auditorium and heartily embraced the pupil who had been elected over him.

Bishop Cannon was a friend of President Carter, and it was a source of great pride to him that he was called to deliver the prayer at the inauguration of the president.

It is impossible to think of Bishop Cannon without recalling Bishop Arthur J. Moore. He was Bishop Moore's "boy" and the bishop loved him as a son. No one rejoiced more in his election than did Bishop Moore, and when Bishop Cannon was sent to Georgia, Bishop Moore's long dream came true at last. Only a relatively short time, however, remained for him to observe the activities of his beloved junior colleague in Georgia, which both of them called home. Another bishop to whom Bishop Cannon was close, and to whom he feels deeply indebted, was Fred Pierce Corson.

The entire Southeastern Jurisdiction expressed its love for Bishop Cannon and its appreciation of him in the erection in 1981 of the William R. Cannon Chapel on the campus of Emory University.

Following Vatican II a new era of ecumenical dialogue was ushered into being, and it continues into the present time. Not only have there been sustained conversations between Roman Catholics and United Methodists but also between United Methodists and other churches. For the past sixteen years the Council of Bishops has looked largely to Bishop Cannon to furnish United Methodist episcopal leadership in such dialogue. Bishop Cannon has been qualified for this responsibility to an extent unmatched by any contemporary United Methodist bishop.

No United Methodist bishop of Bishop Cannon's time exceeded him as a scholar. His major was church history and theology, and he had won his spurs as a Wesleyan theologian long before his election to the episcopacy. The ancient church fathers were very much alive to him, and he would often quote them in sermons or in arguments.

He has to his credit years of seminary teaching. Some of his writings are generally accepted as standards in his field of Wesleyan theology. The intricacies of dogma and the contributions of the theologians of the centuries are like an open book to Bishop Cannon, and the jargon of the sophisticated presents no problem to him.

The *Discipline* (Par. 2404) provides that in formal relations with other churches or ecclesiastical bodies the Council of Bishops shall be the primary liaison for The United Methodist

Church. In its discharge of this responsibility, the council has learned to take advantage of Bishop Cannon's expertise. The World Methodist Council has recognized his possible contribution to ecumenical dialogue and has called upon him for continuing conversations with the Roman Catholic, Lutheran, and Orthodox churches. In 1981 he was elected chairperson of the executive committee of the World Methodist Council.

ALSIE H. CARLETON

Bishop Alsie H. Carleton was elected by the 1968 South Central Jurisdictional Conference. He was at the time professor of church administration at Perkins School of Theology. Previously he had served as pastor in the Northwest Texas Conference and as pastor and district superintendent in the North Texas Conference. He was assigned to the Northwest Texas-New Mexico area, which meant he returned as a bishop to the conference into which he was admitted on trial as a young preacher in 1936. He served this area until his retirement in 1980.

A rather unusual thing occurred connected with his election. Another person receiving votes in that election was Bishop Carleton's brother-in-law, Dr. Finis Crutchfield of Boston Avenue Church in Tulsa. In 1972 Dr. Crutchfield was elected to the episcopacy, and thus the Reverend Finis Crutchfield, Sr., a greatly loved pastor of the North Texas Conference, came to have both a son and a son-in-law in the College of Bishops of the South Central Jurisdiction.

Bishop Carleton is a matter-of-fact man, modest almost to an extreme. He was regular in his attendance at the Council of Bishops, but he seldom spoke unless called upon or given a definite assignment. A change came in the 1968 Council of Bishops to which Bishop Carleton was a striking exception. Prior to that time, it had been customary for newly elected bishops to be seen and not heard during their first quadrennium. According to Bishop McConnell, Bishop Blake had shocked the bishops in 1920 by speaking at the first meeting he attended as a newly elected bishop, and the story of his violation of a tradition in the Board of Bishops was still going the rounds almost a half century later. The class of 1968, however, proved to be quite a vocal group. With the exception of Bishop Carleton, all took the floor at some time and showed no sense of feeling inhibited because of being new. In the sixties many traditions died in the Council of Bishops as well as elsewhere, and most newly elected bishops since then have not hesitated to "dive off the dock" at their first meeting.

Bishop Carleton proved to be an effective administrator. He carried over into his episcopacy the attention to administration that had characterized his teaching days at Perkins. His major interest was his area, and he promoted the area program with dispatch. He traveled its vast distances without giving way to weariness. His area contained a substantial Native American population and a considerable Hispanic population, and he made these a matter of continuing concern.

Bishop Carleton's chief service in the church-at-large was as president of the Board of Pensions from 1972 to 1980. He was fitted for this assignment by both training and natural interest. During his presidency the vast changes in the church's pension program, which were adopted by the 1980 General Conference, were matured.

Upon the bishop's retirement he and Mrs. Carleton continued to make their home in Albuquerque, New Mexico, and the bishop accepted certain promotional responsibilities for McMurry College at Abilene.

CORNELIO M. FERRER

Bishop Cornelio M. Ferrer was elected in the 1968 Philippines Central Conference. He was at the time on the staff of the National Council of Churches of the Philippines. Previously he had served as a pastor, a district superintendent, and a college teacher. He was assigned to the Manila area.

Bishop Ferrer gave careful attention to the details of administration, and he was an acceptable presiding officer. In the part of the church where he served this was no small accomplishment, for nowhere are Methodists greater sticklers for the *Discipline* and parliamentary law than in the Philippines.

Bishop Ferrer's time in the active episcopacy was short. Term episcopacy prevails in the Philippines, and in 1972 he failed of reelection, as did his companion Bishop Granadosin. The Judicial Council ruled that both bishops should continue in office until their successors were elected.

Another Central Conference session was held in 1974 at which time Bishop Ferrer again failed to receive the necessary majority for election, although he came close to it. He took this failure to be reelected in good spirit, realizing how closely the lines were drawn in the body. He was along in years at the time of this Central Conference session, and the Judicial Council eventually ruled that having reached the age he had reached, he was entitled to continue a member of the council as a retired bishop. In retirement Bishop Ferrer has continued his lifelong interest in rural life and has given himself to the development of a new, unique rural enterprise.

PAUL L. A. GRANADOSIN

Bishop Paul L. A. Granadosin was elected by the 1968 Philippine Central Conference. He had been a pastor for some years and was at the time district superintendent of the Manila District. A graduate of both Union Seminary and Garrett, he is one of the gifted ministers of the church in the Philippines. He was assigned to the Baguio area. In 1974 he was reelected and again in 1976. When Bishop Ferrer failed of reelection in 1974, Bishop Granadosin carried both the Baguio and Manila areas for the balance of the quadrennium. When Bishop Mercado, elected in 1976, found it necessary to resign, Bishop Granadosin served both areas for that quadrennium.

Bishop Granadosin is a fervent evangelist who carries his audiences with him. He is an unwearying traveler, covering faithfully the vast island empire represented by two episcopal areas; yet at the same time he has managed to attend the meetings of the council and other gatherings of the larger church.

ABEL T. MUZOREWA

Bishop Abel T. Muzorewa was elected by the 1968 Africa Central Conference. At this conference Bishop Ralph Dodge retired, and the election of Bishop Muzorewa meant that the Africa College of Bishops now had a majority of black bishops for the first time. In four more years the college would become completely African. Prior to his election the bishop had been a teacher, evangelist, pastor, and leader in conference affairs. Bishop Muzorewa was elected to supervise work in Rhodesia (now Zimbabwe) and has continued in this assignment ever since.

The bishop is a product of the missionary enterprise of Methodism of which the church can well be proud. He was born on the grounds of the historic center at Old Umtali, where he went to school. A devoted missionary, Dr. M. J. Murphree, was an influential friend and sponsor. Bishop Muzorewa came to the United States for further study at Central College in Missouri and at Scarritt College in Nashville. He had continuing encouragement from his mentor, Bishop Ralph Dodge, who had been a missionary in Africa, Africa secretary of the Board of Missions, and a bishop in Africa.

Bishop Muzorewa has always defended the rights of his people. He spoke out fearlessly against the oppression of the white minority government and was committed to political action to remedy the situation. He became a leading political activist and an internationally known figure. Finally he witnessed the fall of the Ian Smith regime, and he became the first prime minister of the new Zimbabwe. It was the only time in history that a Methodist bishop had held such an office. He did not resign his episcopal office, but he did ask to be relieved temporarily of its responsibilities. Bishop Ralph Dodge was recalled from retirement to substitute for him.

The premiership did not last long, however. Some persons in the church-at-large criticized the bishop during his premiership because of his attempts at building a biracial society, which they preeceived to be a compromise. When an election finally came, he lost heavily, and national political leadership passed to the hands of others. He once again took up his episcopal duties and continued his efforts to witness the improvement of the lot of his people.

New Leadership for a New Church

ROY C. NICHOLS

Bishop Roy C. Nichols was elected by the 1968 Northeastern Jurisdictional Conference. He was the first black bishop to be elected by a Jurisdictional Conference following the dissolution of the Central Jurisdiction. Subsequently, the Northeastern Jurisdiction was to elect Bishops Carroll and Skeete; the North Central Bishop Ammons; the South Central Bishops Dixon and Handy; and the Western Bishop Talbert. But to Bishop Nichols belongs the honor of being the first black bishop elected in what is now The United Methodist Church. At the time of his election, Bishop Nichols was pastor of Salem Church, New York; previously he had served in California. He was assigned to the Pittsburgh area, which he served until 1980 when he was transferred to the New York area.

In the 1968 General Conference Bishop Nichols an active floor figure, and he exerted much effort to bring into being the Commission on Religion and Race. He became at once a vocal member of the council. He entered readily into council debates and often made amending motions or took exception to a motion before the house. He has an incisive mind and can see quickly the possible implications in a proposed course of action. He has a habit of carefully assembling data and making extensive notes, which he uses for reinforcement of what he says when he takes the floor. He was not too impressed with the general pattern of operation of the council when he came into it, and he was one of the bishops strongly advocating the changes represented in the present pattern of operation. The bishop's fairness is reflected often not only in his willingness but also his eagerness to hear all sides of a question.

Bishop Nichols is a gifted preacher. His sermons are scriptural, informative, pertinent to the day, provocative, and moving. He has an appreciation of the dramatic that enables him to add a little something extra to a situation. Those who were present will never forget the moving way in which he brought the 1980 General Conference to a close. The bishops themselves can never forget the tender way he handled matters on the evening in Houston when the council said farewell to the bishops from India, who because of the coming of the autonomous church would no longer be council members.

Bishop Nichols has been entrusted with large responsibility by the church. He represented The United Methodist Church on the Central Committee of the World Council of Churches, where he proved to be a vocal member. For a period he was the president of the World Division of the Board of Global Ministries. Often he was sent by the council on significant missions, especially in Africa, and he was one of the fathers of the African Emphasis scheduled for 1980–1984 quadrennium. Bishop Nichols was the president of the Council of Bishops from 1980 to 1981.

CARL ERNST SOMMER

Bishop Carl Ernst Sommer was elected by the 1968 Germany Central Conference. He was at the time dean of the seminary at Frankfurt and had spent most of his ministry in educational work. He was the son of Bishop J. W. E. Sommer, who was bishop of Germany from 1946 to his death in 1953. The Sommers represented one of two father-and-son teams in the Methodist episcopacy; the other was Bishop Matthew W. Clair elected in 1920 and Bishop Matthew W. Clair, Jr., elected in 1952.

Bishop Sommer went by his middle name, Ernst. He limited his attendance at meetings of the council, always being anxious to spare the church expense. In line with his becoming modesty, he was comitted to a simple life-style. He saw service in the German army, as had his predecessor, Bishop Friedrich Wunderlich.

Bishop Sommer belonged to the scholarly ranks of the episcopacy. He read widely and devoted himself to considerable writing. The whole field of Christian education was a major interest for him.

When Bishop Sommer began his administration, all the German conferences were under his supervision as they had been under his predecessors—Bishops Wunderlich, Sommer, Sr., and Melle. This was to be the case for him for only a brief time, however, since in 1970 the conference in the German Democratic Republic was set up as a separate Central

Conference with Bishop Armin Härtel elected as administrator.

Bishop Sommer retired in 1977, and he and Mrs. Sommer continued to make their home in Frankfurt, where he died in 1981.

D. FREDERICK WERTZ

Bishop D. Frederich Wertz was elected by the 1968 Northeastern Jurisdictional Conference. He was at the time president of Lycoming College. Previously he had served as pastor and district superintendent in the Central Pennsylvania Conference. He was assigned to the West Virginia area, which he served until 1980 when he was transferred to the Washington area.

Bishop Wertz belongs to the liberal school and is an apostle of change. He does not subscribe to change merely for change's sake, but he believes that changes have to come in society as a whole and also in the church. As an administrator in the college world during the sixties, he had lived with pressures and pressure groups and had learned how to cope with such things. He came into the Council of Bishops at a time when the council was feeling for the first time such pressures, including disruption of its meetings and demands for hearings by various pressure groups, some of whom were extreme in their tactics and demands. The bishop urged the council to take such experiences in stride and center its attention upon the conditions that lay behind such protests so that remedies could be found.

Bishop Wertz has a keen social conscience and is an outspoken defender of the exploited, the oppressed, the disenfranchised, and the poor. He is committed to the building of a just society, and he has labored to that end through his activities in the Commission on Religion and Race and in the Board of Global Ministries of which he was the president for a four-year period.

Bishop Wertz has been concerned about a properly qualified ministry for the church. He was a member of the Commission on the Ministry which recommended to the 1968 General Conference far-reaching changes in the legislation on the ministry. As a member of the Council of Bishops he was much interested in the orientation experience planned quadrennially for newly elected bishops. This orientation experience had been originated by Bishop Baker in 1948 and was held at first in connection with a regular meeting of the council. Later it was held separately. Finally under the leadership of Bishop Wertz, further changes were made in the program, and the wives of the newly elected bishops were included in the experience.

Bishop Wertz was an effective presiding officer when called to occupy the chair at General Conference.

JOSEPH R. LANCE

Bishop Joseph R. Lance was elected by the 1968 Central Conference of Southern Asia. He was at the time executive secretary of the council of Christian Social Concerns for the Methodist Church in India. Previously he had been a pastor and a chaplain. He was assigned to the Lucknow area to which he was reassigned at succeeding Central Conferences.

Bishop Lance is well trained, having studied in India and then having gone as a Crusade Scholar to Garrett where he spent three years. Indian Methodism is in his blood; his father was a minister before him.

Bishop Lance proved to be a prophet of the new Day. Although he had the fullest appreciation of the missionary heritage, he felt that the time had come for the "Indianization" of the church in India. To this end he was committed to autonomy. When the bishops from India met for the last time with the Council of Bishops at Houston in the fall of 1980 he spoke for Indian Methodism at the farewell service. In the new autonomous church he was assigned to the Delhi area.

ERIC MITCHELL

Bishop Eric Mitchel was elected by the 1968 Southern Asia Central Conference. He had been a pastor, a district superintendent, and a leader in conference activities. He was assigned to the Hyderabad area from which he went in 1976 to the Delhi area.

The bishop can express himself readily on the platform or in debate. He has a solid educational background; he graduated from Leonard Theological Seminary and did graduate work as a Crusade Scholar at Union Seminary, New York. In the Council meetings he usually offered a well-reasoned contribution to discussions.

Bishop Mitchell is committed to the advancement of the mission of the church, looks to the future, and seems undaunted by change. He was an ardent advocate of full support of its ministry by the national church and of the freedom of the church in India to direct its own affairs.

FEDERICO J. PAGURA

Bishop Federico J. Pagura was elected by the 1969 session of the Latin American Central Conference held in Santiago, Chile. This was the last session of that Central Conference. The churches in Argentina, Chile, Bolivia, Uraguay, and Peru had all chosen to become autonomous and to elect their own bishops or executive officers. Only Panama and Costa Rica remained, and Bishop Pagura was elected to provide episcopal supervision for them. He was not present at the time of election but arrived for the consecration service.

Bishop Pagura's term as a bishop of The United Methodist Church was brief because within a short time the churches in both Panama and Costa Rica entered into church unions. A few years later he was elected bishop of the Methodist Church of Argentina. Thus he established the record of being a bishop in two churches.

Bishop Pagura is a scholarly man who has spent much of his life in seminary teaching. He is widely known in Latin America and has had a prominent role in ecumenical affairs. He has been an avid defender of human rights, an advocate of high educational standards for the ministry and the laity, and a sponsor of continuing mutual sharing upon the part of the Methodist churches in Latin America with the mother United Methodist Church.

OLE E. BORGEN

Bishop Ole E. Borgen was elected by a special session of the Northern Europe Central Conference called in 1970, following the death of Bishop Odd Hagen. He had served as assistant to Bishop Hagen and had also seen a period of service with the Geneva office of the Methodist World Council. The area which he was elected to supervise included Sweden, Norway, Denmark, Finland, Latvia, and Estonia.

Bishop Borgen loves music and he became the pianist for the Council of Bishops when Bishop Ledden was no longer able to serve in that capacity. He is a linguist, speaking several languages in addition to his native tongue.

The bishop is well trained. After his schooling in his native land, he studied in the United States and received a B. D. degree at Duke University and a Ph.D. degree from Drew University. He first joined the Western North Carolina Conference, but transferred to his native Norway Conference in 1966.

Bishop Borgen is a scholarly man. He majored in theology, particularly Wesleyan theology, and several works he has written in that field have enjoyed a commendable response.

Bishop Borgen has not followed the pattern of most earlier Central Conference bishops who limited their attendance at the council; he regularly attends its meetings. He is an unwearying traveler of not only his own area but also the globe if assigned responsibilities call for such travel.

The bishop became the most vocal of the Central Conference bishops and a natural leader among them. To understand his position fully, one must look back to the 1964–1968 quadrennium when, under the direction of the Commission on the Structure of Methodism Overseas, consideration was given to the question of whether the world church pattern should continue or whether the formation of autonomous national churches was more desirable.

In the various conversations held during the quadrennium a division of opinion evolved among the Methodist churches overseas from the United States. Latin America, Southeast Asia, Taiwan, and Southern Asia inclined toward the autonomous church pattern. But the churches in Europe felt differently. They felt there was great advantage in continuing as a part of a world church insofar as they represented tiny minorities in their own lands. Matters came to head in a conference at Atlantic City prior to the 1968 General Conference. There Bishop Borgen led the battle for those conferences overseas from the United States who favored continuance of the world church pattern.

It was logical therefore that Bishop Borgen should insist that the Central Conference bishops who chose to remain with the mother church should share fully in all that happened in the council. He has an alert mind and has become a monitor for Central Conference interests. He is quick to take exception to anything he thinks is not fair to, or might subtract from, the interests of the Central conferences. In 1984 he was elected president-designate to the Council.

ARMIN E. HÄRTEL

Bishop Armin E. Härtel was elected by the 1970 Central Conference of the German Democratic Republic. At the time he was a district superintendent. He was reelected at subsequent sessions of the Central Conference. He was the first Methodist bishop elected in a socialist state.

Bishop Härtel has been devoted to the work of his area. Life in his country is lived under some restrictions, but the bishop maintained that the church is free to prosecute its essential mission. He maintains the traditional emphasis of German Methodism upon personal piety and devotion to good works. He is fully committed to social justice, particularly to the realization of the dream of a peaceful world.

VII
ADDITIONS TO THE EPISCOPAL LEADERSHIP TEAM, 1972–1976

The beginning of the second quadrennium of the life of The United Methodist Church witnessed the retirement of eighteen bishops. Four of these each had twenty-four years of active service in the Council. The group as a whole had two hundred seventy-five years of active service. This meant, of course, a large turnover in the personnel of the Council, as in the various jurisdictional and central conferences new bishops were elected to fill the vacancies.

JAMES M. AULT

Bishop James M. Ault was elected by the 1972 Northeastern Jurisdictional Conference. At the time he was the dean of Drew Theological Seminary. He was one of three seminary officers elected that year, the others were Bishop Mack B. Stokes, associate dean at Candler, and Bishop Wayne Clymer, president of Evangelical Seminary. He was the next Drew faculty member to be elected to the episcopacy after the election of Bishop Hazen G. Werner in 1948 and the latest of a line of Drew faculty contributions to the episcopacy.

Before his deanship at Drew, Bishop Ault had been dean of students and professor of practical theology at Union Seminary, New York. Prior to that he had served pastorates in Massachusetts and New Jersey. His conference membership was in the Northern New Jersey Conference. He was assigned to the Philadelphia area, which included the Eastern Pennsylvania, Wyoming, and Puerto Rico Conferences. He served this area for eight years and in 1980 was transferred to the Pittsburgh area.

Bishop Ault is methodical and gives careful attention to detail. Papers that come from his hand bear the marks of the scholar. He has pronounced social convictions to which he is quietly and fearlessly loyal. Until he became secretary he seldom spoke up in the Council of Bishops, but when he did speak it was to the point and the papers he presented were carefully refined and documented.

It is only natural that with his experience in a faculty position in two of the country's great seminaries, one of his major interests should be the training of the ministry. He was an obvious choice for the chairmanship of the Division of the Ordained Ministry of the Board of Higher Education for the 1976–1980 quadrennium. This quadrennium witnessed significant changes in the legislation regarding the ministry, and the bishop was much involved in them.

In 1980 Bishop Ault was elected secretary of the Council of Bishops, succeeding Bishop James K. Mathews who had reached retirement.

ROBERT M. BLACKBURN

Bishop Robert M. Blackburn was elected by the 1972 Southeastern Jurisdictional Conference. At the time he was pastor of First Church, Orlando, Florida. All his previous pastorates had been in the Florida Conference. His father had been a member of the Florida Conference and had done pioneer work, especially in south Florida. His brother, Dr. Henry Blackburn, was a vigorous leader in the Florida Conference and received a substantial vote for the episcopacy in 1960. The bishop was assigned to the Raleigh area, which he served until 1980 when he was transferred to the Richmond area.

Bishop Blackburn has keen powers of observation and analysis which enable him to size up situations and arrive at his own conclusions. He is a thoughtful preacher whose messages bear testimony to carefulness of preparation and insight into truth.

Bishop Blackburn has been a less vocal member of the Council of Bishops. In his modesty he does not put himself forward, but the council soon discovered his native and acquired ability and learned it could place a high degree of trust in him.

EDWARD G. CARROLL

Bishop Edward G. Carroll was elected by the 1972 Northeastern Jurisdictional Conference. He was the second black bishop to be elected by a Northeastern Jurisdictional Conference; the first was Bishop Roy Nichols. With Bishop Prince Albert Taylor still on the active list, the election of Bishop Carroll meant that one-third of the bishops of that jurisdiction during the 1972–1976 quadrennium was black.

Bishop Carroll had served in the old Washington Conference prior to conference merger in 1968 and in the Baltimore Conference after that time. There he was appointed by Bishop John Wesley Lord to the Marvin Memorial Church in Silver Springs, Maryland, a predominantly white congregation named for Bishop Enoch M. Marvin, one of the great bishops of the Methodist Episcopal Church, South, and in an earlier day one of the outstanding churches of the southern church. This was one of the early appointments across racial lines, and Bishop Carroll proved that a transracial appointment could be effective. Bishop Carroll was assigned to the Boston area where he served until retirement in 1980.

Bishop Carroll proved adept at dealing with tension. He demonstrated this ability in the Washington and Baltimore Conferences, and again in his administration of the Boston area during particularly difficult days. His quiet loyalty to his convictions, his willingness to listen to others, his fair-minded effort to maintain objectivity, and his unwillingness to dodge problems, all contributed to making him a helpful agent for the resolution of conflict.

The bishop greatly enjoyed travel and in his eight years of active service became well acquainted with much of the global operation of the church.

Upon his retirement in 1980, he and Mrs. Carroll continued to make their home in Boston.

Additions to the Episcopal Leadership Team, 1972–1976

EMILIO DE CARVALHO

Bishop Emilio de Carvalho was elected by the 1972 Africa Central Conference and assigned to Angola. Prior to his election he had been a professor and principal of Emmanuel Seminary. He was the first citizen of Angola to be elected to the episcopacy in The United Methodist Church or its predecessor bodies and the first native black bishop to supervise the Angola work. Native black bishops had already supervised the work in Zaire, Mozambique, and Zimbabwe, but not Angola.

When Bishop de Carvalho would address the Council of Bishops on matters that concerned his continent, he would usually write out carefully what he had to say and deliver it in a soft-spoke voice. In the meetings he would advocate the fullest social application of the gospel and plead persuasively for an understanding of the situation in his own and other African countries that have suffered for centuries from colonialism and exploitation. Only recently have they come to know the privilege of self-government. He is a striking representative of a new day.

WILBUR W. Y. CHOY

Bishop Wilbur W. Y. Choy was elected by the 1972 Western Jurisdictional Conference. His election was unique in that it represented the first time that a person coming from the Asian minority in the United States had been elected a bishop in The United Methodist Church or its predecessor bodies. Asians had been elected in Central Conferences in China, the Philippines, and India, but not in the United States. Also Asians had been elected in autonomous churches springing from the original Methodist parent body in Korea, Malaysia, Sumatra, Burma, Singapore, and Taiwan.

At the time of his election, Bishop Choy was a district superintendent in the California-Nevada Conference. Originally he had joined the California Oriental Provisional Conference in 1949. This conference was merged with the California-Nevada Conference in 1952. Bishop Choy had been one of "Bishop Baker's boys." He was assigned to the

Seattle area to which he was reassigned in 1976. In 1980 he was assigned to the San Francisco area, this assignment putting him near the heart of the Asian constituency on the West Coast.

The bishop has been active in the growing group in Methodism concerned about Asian affairs. In his earlier ministry he witnessed the dissolution of the Oriental work and its merger into the surrounding geographic conferences. Now he has lived to see a new day with older Asian churches in the States springing into new life; with a rising tide of immigration from Korea, the Philippines, Vietnam, and other Asian countries; and with the widespread call for the organization of new churches for Koreans and other Orientals in cities which heretofore have had no significant Asian population. In this rebirth of Asian Methodism in the United States, Bishop Choy has played a happy and effective role.

In 1982 he was elected president-designate of the Council of Bishops.

WAYNE K. CLYMER

Bishop Wayne K. Clymer was elected by the 1972 North Central Jurisdictional Conference. He was at the time president of Evangelical Theological Seminary at Naperville, Illinois, where he had served as a faculty member for twenty-one years before being elected president. He was the second former Evangelical United Brethren minister to be elected to the episcopacy after union in 1968. With his election at the time of Bishop Reuben H. Mueller's retirement, the number of former Evangelical United Brethren bishops in the North Central Jurisdiction remained at two, and the other being Bishop Paul A. Washburn. When Bishop Washburn retired in 1980, the number of active former Evangelical United Brethren Bishops in the college of the jurisdiction dropped to one. Bishop Clymer was assigned to the Minnesota area where he served for eight years. In 1980 he was transferred to the Iowa area.

Bishop Clymer has a theological mind, a theological commitment, and a theologian's approach to matters. He is a careful student, fully knowledgeable in the theological field.

Additions to the Episcopal Leadership Team, 1972–1976

He does not quote the ancient church fathers to the extent that his colleague Bishop Cannon is prone to do, but nevertheless he knows them well. He has the ability to express his thoughts effectively, and on more than one occasion in the Council of Bishops he has given a striking demonstration of being able to think upon his feet. When given an assignment, he would carefully marshal the facts necessary to sustain his position, and he expressed himself forthrightly and candidly. At the same time he sought to be understanding of the viewpoints of others and to be fair in his appraisals.

In the episcopacy Bishop Clymer has remained the teacher. The Committee on Teaching Concerns of the council appealed to him, and he served as its effective chairman for a period.

Another of Bishop Clymer's major interests is what has long been called "overseas relief." He was for some years identified with the United Methodist Committee on Overseas Relief. He made a number of visits to some places where the world's hunger situation was most evident, such as Cambodia, and returned to plead the cause of the hungry. He preached that while it is true that man cannot live by bread alone, no one of God's children can live without bread. When he was the host of the Council of Bishops in Minneapolis, he demonstrated his concern by omitting the usual formal dinner and having instead a public service to which United Methodists came from all over Minnesota to bring an offering in a staggering amount designated for world hunger.

FINIS A. CRUTCHFIELD, JR.

Bishop Finis A. Crutchfield, Jr., was elected by the 1972 South Central Jurisdictional Conference. He was at the time pastor of Boston Avenue Church, Tulsa, Oklahoma, the same church from which Bishop Paul V. Galloway was elected before him in 1960 and Bishop J. Chess Lovern after him in 1976. He was a son of the parsonage; his father the Reverend Finis Crutchfield, Sr., had been a greatly beloved Texas preacher. He was a brother-in-law of Bishop Alsie H. Carleton who was elected four years before he was. He was assigned to the New Orleans area, which he served until 1976 when he was transferred to the Houston area.

Bishop Crutchfield is characterized by his matter-of-fact approach to situations and his preference for practical, commonsense solutions. He is rigidly honest, and he refuses to hide what he feels or believes. Rather he dares to ask questions and to speak up freely and forthrightly. No bishop has sought more faithfully to secure a generous response to genuine needs. The Houston area represents one of the areas of United Methodism with the largest resources, and the bishop has found sheer delight in encouraging his people to respond generously to the calls of the kingdom.

Some persons consider Bishop Crutchfield to be perhaps a bit conservative, which he is, compared to some of his episcopal colleagues. But his is a healthy, legitimate conservatism. He cherishes his Wesleyan heritage, and he is unwilling to surrender his commitment to its basic emphasis. He cherishes traditional values long stressed by Methodism, and he is fully committed to doing battle for them if necessary. In the Council of Bishops and in the boards of the church to which he was assigned, he took his stand courageously. He is not averse to change, but he is averse to change merely for change's sake. Living in a changing world and having administrative responsibility in a church also changing, he has sought to follow the admonition of Paul, "Prove all things. Hold fast to that which is good."

In 1982 he was elected president of the Council of Bishops.

JESSE R. DEWITT

Bishop Jesse R. DeWitt was elected by the 1972 North Central Jurisdictional Conference. At the time he was an associate general secretary of the National Division of the Board of Global Ministries. While attending Garrett he served a student charge in the old Rock River Conference. He joined the Detroit Conference where he wrote a record, as an urban district superintendent called upon to handle crisis situations, that attracted considerable attention. He was assigned to the Wisconsin area where he served for eight years. In 1980 he was transferred to the Chicago area comprised of the conference in which he began his student ministry some thirty years before, plus the former Evangelical

Additions to the Episcopal Leadership Team, 1972–1976

United Brethren churches of the same geographic area, all now united into the Northern Illinois Conference of The United Methodist Church.

Bishop DeWitt has represented, as have several of his colleagues elected in the same general period, something of a new brand of bishop. He is somewhat more to the left than some bishops, and he sometimes surprises his older brethren by the positions he takes. He is committed to change. Generally, he has supported advance positions on matters under consideration by the council.

He is willing to experiment with new ways of doing things whether it is in appointment making, conference operation, or the functions of the Council of Bishops. He strongly advocates full recognition of the ministry of women at every level, of minority empowerment, and of full rights for all God's children. He is perhaps inclined toward greater tolerance of ministers and lay persons who do not adhere to long-accepted patterns than are some bishops.

Bishop DeWitt is particularly helpful in resolving conflicts and in dealing with urban problems. He is concerned about all current social issues and can not rest until he feels he is doing all within his power to contribute to bringing into being the better society of which he has dreamed.

ERNEST T. DIXON, JR.

Bishop Ernest T. Dixon, Jr., was elected by the 1972 South Central Jurisdictional Conference. At the time he was serving on the staff of the General Program Council of the church. Previously he had been a staff member of the General Board of Education and of Tuskegee Institute, had had several pastorates in Texas, and had been president of Philander Smith College. He was the first black to be elected by the South Central Jurisdiction, his election to be followed in 1980 by that of Bishop W. T. Handy, Jr. He was assigned to the Kansas area where he served until 1980 at which time he was transferred to the San Antonio area, thus becoming the bishop of the city of his birth.

Bishop Dixon has an interest in all developments in the life of the church, but his special interest is in the local church. In his administration of the Kansas area he gave large attention to this matter. He is also concerned about higher education, particularly in the black colleges. He has sponsored and advocated the establishment and promotion of the Black College Fund and was chairman of the Committee on Black Colleges. He was president of the Board of Higher Education from 1972 to 1976. He is an outspoken defender of the rights of his people and of all other people. His assignment to the San Antonio area associated him with another minority in United Methodism, the Hispanics, for he became the bishop of the Rio Grande Conference, the one entirely Hispanic conference in the United States.

FAMA ONEMA

Bishop Fama Onema was elected at the 1972 African Central Conference. He was at the time a professor in the seminary. He was assigned to the Zaire area. The 1972 elections meant that the time had come at last when all four episcopal areas of the Central Conference had a native African as their bishop.

The bishop has regularly attended the meetings of the council where he listens patiently to the lengthy agenda, so much of which necessarily deals with matters more related to the work of the church in the United States. He would report on his work or lead a devotional when called upon. At the 1976 and 1980 Central Conferences he was reelected.

ROBERT E. GOODRICH, JR.

Bishop Robert E. Goodrich, Jr., was elected by the 1972 South Central Jurisdictional Conference. He was at the time the pastor of First Church, Dallas, where he had served for twenty-six years. From this same church Bishop W. Angie Smith was elected in 1944, and Bishop Benjamin R. Oliphint in 1980. Bishop Goodrich was a son of the parsonage; his father, Dr. Robert E. Goodrich, Sr., was one of the prominent downtown preachers of the Methodist Episcopal Church, South, as was his father-in-law, Dr. Paul Quillian. He

Additions to the Episcopal Leadership Team, 1972–1976

was assigned to the Missouri area, which he served until his retirement in 1980.

In the Council of Bishops Bishop Goodrich played mostly a listening role, taking the floor only occasionally or when given some assignment. Prior to his election to the episcopacy, he often played a leading role in General Conference as a committee chairman. In the 1972 General Conference he was chairman of the important Committee of Chairmen, which was responsible for steering the General Conference to the completion of its work. In this capacity he moved efficiently and wisely. The same efficiency marked his operation as an area bishop.

Bishop Goodrich was always in demand as a preacher. A widely known, unique downtown preacher, he provided for the downtown church a magnetic pulpit that could attract people from over a wide metropolitan area. He knew that people would not pass by several neighborhood churches to go downtown to see someone light a candle or to hear a conventional, perhaps carefully prepared but unmoving, sermon. At the same time, he knew that the downtown church could not depend upon the pulpit alone, and he worked to develop a local church program that represented a multifaceted ministry.

The bishop's sermons have their own particular appeal. They make the Scriptures come alive and demonstrate an effective use of the imagination. They have a marked warmth and are sprinkled with human interest material. Taken all together, they invite a response of the will. The bishop has exhibited no theatrical or bombastic tendencies that have been witnessed in some dynamic pulpit personalities. His episcopal colleagues frequently call upon him to fill the role of conference preacher. He has been effective as a radio and television preacher, and he knows how to reach a vast unseen audience through these media.

Bishop Goodrich retired in 1980, and he and Mrs. Goodrich moved to Houston, Texas, where the bishop joined the staff of St. Luke's Church to continue once again a ministry in a large church situation, this time in a supporting role.

DON W. HOLTER

Bishop Don W. Holter was elected by the 1972 South Central Jurisdictional Conference. He was at the time president of St. Paul Theological Seminary. In early life he had joined the Kansas Conference and had then gone as a missionary to the Philippines where he served for some years, part of the time as president of the seminary. He was in the Philippines during World War II and was interned for three years by the Japanese. He was a professor at Garrett before going to St. Paul in 1958. His election was a high tribute to him because he could serve only four years because of his age. He was assigned to the Nebraska area.

Bishop Holter is marked by graciousness and a fully democratic spirit. His good judgment and fine sense of balance had made him valuable for difficult assignments in the general church prior to his election as bishop. He could present a highly debatable report in a quiet, steady manner, answer questions, defend its proposals, and see it through to its adoption. Naturally, one of his major interests has been the ministry, and much of the current legislation regarding the ministry bears the marks of his influence, as do current plans for the church's support of theological education.

Bishop Holter's term of active service was confined to four years. He retired in 1976, and he and Mrs. Holter have made their home in Prairie Village, Kansas.

JOEL D. MCDAVID

Bishop Joel D. McDavid was elected by the 1972 Southeastern Jurisdictional Conference. At the time he was pastor of Dauphin Way Church, Mobile, and prior to that he had served various pastorates in the Alabama-West Florida Conference. During the 1968–1972 quadrennium he served as the secretary in the Committee on Restructure of Boards and Agencies and proved himself in many ways a balance wheel of the committee. He was assigned to the Florida area where he remained for eight years. In 1980 he was transferred to the Atlanta area.

Bishop McDavid's thoughtfulness and attention to detail

Additions to the Episcopal Leadership Team, 1972–1976

made him a good choice by the council to care for the Bishops Courtesy Fund and the many remembrances in hours of illness, sorrow, or rejoicing in the episcopal family that the administration of the fund involves.

One of Bishop McDavid's major concerns has been the local church. He believes that United Methodism as a whole can not rise above the sum total of its local churches. For eight years he took leadership in the Board of Discipleship in the Division of Education. He is fully committed to local church growth, local church efficiency, and local church extension. He favors evangelism, and any decline of emphasis upon it by the ministers or churches deeply disturbs his soul. In his assignment to Florida he found himself in one of the sections of the church enjoying the highest percentage of growth, and he gave well-planned guidance to a church extension program there.

During the days of his administration Florida received the great influx of Spanish-speaking immigrants, chiefly from Cuba but also from other Caribbean islands. This immigration meant operating in a new context for society and for the church, particularly in South Florida. The bishop sought to deal creatively and helpfully in this situation, and the Florida Conference responded to his leadership. Programs to meet the basic physical needs of refugees and to help them adjust to a new life situation were developed. In some churches in neighborhoods where there were numerous Spanish-speaking residents, second congregations where developed to meet at separate hours from the English-speaking congregation. In some cases where the Hispanic concentration was high, entire former English-speaking churches were transformed into Spanish-speaking churches. A number of former pastors in the Cuba Conference who were forced out of Cuba under the Castro regime became members of the Florida Conference and served the new Hispanic work.

With his transfer to Georgia, Bishop McDavid was to find himself in a quite different situation from what he had known in his first episcopal assignment. There would be no such population growth as in Florida, nor the tourists, nor the Hispanic influx, but there would be work to do, problems to solve, and people to serve, all in a setting that included Emory University with its rich memories of his student days.

M. ELIA PETER

Bishop M. Elia Peter was elected by the 1972 Central Conference of Southern Asia and was assigned to the Hyderabad area.

The devotional messages which Bishop Peter brought to the Council of Bishops on several occasions displayed thoughtfulness, insight, and concern for the application of the gospel to all of life. He was committed to the Indianization of the church in India in the interest of its greater effectiveness. For eight years he served as a United Methodist bishop, but in 1980 he became one of the bishops of the new autonomous Church of India. He was assigned to the newly established Bangalore area.

FRANK L. ROBERTSON

Bishop Frank L. Robertson was elected by the 1972 Southeastern Jurisdictional Conference. At the time he was pastor of First Church, Valdosta, Georgia. He was a favorite son of the South Georgia Conference where he had been a district superintendent and pastor of some of the larger churches. He was assigned to the Louisville area where he served for eight years. In 1980 he was transferred to the Birmingham area.

Throughout most of his ministry in South Georgia, he had only one bishop, Arthur J. Moore, himself a South Georgian. Bishop Moore was devoted to him and he to Bishop Moore. For the last twelve years of his ministry in the South Georgia Conference, his bishop was John Owen Smith, who also was greatly attached to him, and he shared much of Bishop Smith's democratic attitude and optimism.

Bishop Robertson faced some difficult situations, including a strike at the Pikeville Hospital which came almost the very week of his assignment to Kentucky. The strikers appealed to the Council of Bishops as well as to other church agencies. While the Council of Bishops had no power in the situation,

Additions to the Episcopal Leadership Team, 1972–1976

there was in the council sympathy for the strikers, as there was also in the General Board of Social Concerns. The council appointed a committee to work with Bishop Robertson composed of Bishops Allen, Holter, and Wicke. Bishop Robertson as a fledgling bishop was caught between the strikers, the Pikeville community, the trustees of the hospital, the Council of Bishops, the Board of Social Concerns, and the Church press. Through it all he maintained a calm equilibrium and sought to be fair to all concerned.

The bishop is a good presiding officer, able to keep in quiet command of whatever body he is called to preside over. He knows how to clarify a motion before the house and to handle with dispatch any amendments attached to it.

The bishop chose to make his a pastoral episcopacy, and he gives himsef with devotion to his area. One of his conferences was the Red Bird Mission, a project of the former Evangelical United Brethren Church in the Kentucky mountains. Red Bird had large appeal to the bishop's heart, and no more effective project was to be found in all Appalachia than the Red Bird work.

In the Council of Bishops Bishop Robertson has been given assignments from time to time, such as one on the Program Committee of the General Conference which he carried through with efficiency. He served for a period as the chairman of the important Committee on Pastoral Concerns of the council.

CARL J. SANDERS

Bishop Carl J. Sanders was elected by the 1972 Southeastern Jurisdictional Conference. He had come near election four years before that time. He was a favorite son of the Virginia Conference, where he had served for some years as pastor and as district superintendent of the Petersburg, Richmond, and Norfolk Districts. At the time of his election he was pastor at Arlington, Virginia. He had been active in the Southeastern Jurisdictional Council and had been one of its officers for some time. He was assigned to the Birmingham area, which he administered for eight years until his retirement in 1980.

Bishop Sanders is a gifted preacher. His sermons are biblical, forceful, well illustrated, and persuasive. When he stands in the pulpit and reads the Scriptures prior to his message, by his striking appearance and effective reading he is already well under way even before the message itself. In this respect he has reminded some older Methodists of Bishop Mouzon of another day.

One of Bishop Sander's great concerns has been evangelism. He regrets any redefining of evangelism that make it anything less than the winning of disciples and helping them to grow in the Christian life. To see United Methodism showing membership losses year after year and registering a decline in professions of faith has weighed on his heart, and he has tried to do something about it. In his active episcopacy he urged upon his preachers and lay people the necessity of a passionate evangelism and promoted well-planned programs of evangelism in his conferences. Better still, he set an example of evangelism.

A companion concern has been for the relief of human suffering, particularly hunger. For four years he was the chairman of the United Methodist Committee on Overseas Relief. He gave much time to this assignment, traveled to parts of the world where the hunger crisis was most acute, saw it with his own eyes, and returned home to tell dramatically the story of what he had seen. He appealed to people who had no personal experience of real hunger to give generously for a hungry world.

Bishop Sanders was one of the bishops assigned to a Deep South area at the time of the dissolution of the Central Jurisdiction and the consolidation of the racial conferences with the geographical conferences. He gave himself to this responsibility in good conscience and sought to be the bishop of all churches and all people.

When Bishop Sanders retired, he and Mrs. Sanders moved to Dothan, Alabama, to a home provided for them by Alabama Methodists as a token of their love. The bishop has continued to accept preaching engagements and to devote much of his time to the promotion of the Alabama Methodist Foundation.

Additions to the Episcopal Leadership Team, 1972–1976

MACK B. STOKES

Bishop Mack B. Stokes was elected by the 1972 Southeastern Jurisdictional Conference. He was at the time associate dean of Candler School of Theology where he had been a member of the faculty for thirty-one years. His conference membership was in the Holston Conference. Though he never served a charge in that conference, he was active in its affairs, and he was greatly appreciated and loved and was regularly included in its General Conference delegation. He was assigned to the Jackson area, which he served for eight years until his retirement in 1980.

Bishop Stokes has the bright, questioning eyes of a seeker after truth, and he relishes quiet hours of retreat, study, and writing. The bishop was born in Korea of missionary parents who had a long and distinguished career there and later a brief career in Cuba. They gave to the church four preacher sons. There is something of the missionary about the bishop in his concern for people, his philosophy of service, and his devotion to his own personal mission.

Bishop Stokes was assigned to the Jackson, Mississippi, area at the time when merger of the four black and white conferences was still in process. The merger of the work had begun under the leadership of Bishop Pendergrass four years before. Bishop Stokes found himself the bishop of many black Methodists who had lost a conference identity that meant much to them and who were now wondering about the future. He was also the bishop of white Methodists, some of whom were conservative on racial matters and others were inclined to a more liberal position. Some features of a plan of conference operation which he at first proposed did not prove to be within the law of the church and had to be reconsidered. Eventually, matters were worked through satisfactorily.

Bishop Stokes is a theological scholar who can present profound theological ideas in a form which lay people can grasp. His viewpoint is generally conservative but not reactionary. His chief field of interest has been Wesleyan theology, and he is its avid defender and interpreter. In his preaching he has remained the teacher, and the pulpit is for him a podium. He found time to administer his episcopal duties and to continue his writing as he had done during his teaching days in the seminary, and the eight years of his active episcopacy saw him publish seven books.

Bishop Stokes retired in 1980, and he and Mrs. Stokes moved to Tulsa, Oklahoma, where he became associate dean for doctrinal studies and professor of theology at the School of Religion of Oral Roberts University.

JACK M. TUELL

Bishop Jack M. Tuell was elected by the 1972 Western Jurisdictional Conference. He had been a leader in the Pacific Northwest Conference and was at the time pastor of First Church, Vancouver, Washington. Previously he had been a district superintendent in the Pacific Northwest Conference. He was assigned to the Portland area, so that his move from his place of residence when elected to his first area assignment was an unusually short one. The Portland area included the work in Oregon, part of Idaho, and Alaska. Bishop Tuell served this area for eight years and in 1980 was transferred to the Los Angeles area.

Bishop Tuell is inclined toward new ways of thinking and new approaches to old problems. He advocates greater participation of women at all levels of the ministry and the church's life, and he is an equally ardent supporter of full privileges for the various minorities of the denomination. While he is by nature a sponsor of what he sees as needed change, at the same time he recognizes fully the value of much that is old and maintains a balance in his thinking between the two.

Bishop Tuell was a familiar figure in the church-at-large prior to his election to the episcopacy because he had been a General Conference delegate—and a vocal one at that. By their incisiveness, keen interest in debate, and inclination toward full participation, a few delegates fall into the role of floor leaders. Bishop Tuell belonged in this category. Not only did he prove himself a floor leader, but he also was given important committee assignments because it was recognized he would do the job with thoroughness.

Bishop Tuell was trained originally as a lawyer, and his training benefited the church when he joined the ranks of the

ADDITIONS TO THE EPISCOPAL LEADERSHIP TEAM, 1972–1976

episcopacy. He found himself given important assignments by the Council of Bishops much earlier than are most newly elected bishops. His legal training and analytical mind were almost immediately called upon for assignments related to law and administration. He has been adept at spotting law in the *Discipline* that needs to be rewritten or replaced or seems to be in conflict with the Constitution. The bishop has been recognized as one of the most effective presiding officers in the council.

By the time Bishop Tuell had been a bishop for only eight years, he had been called upon to deal with two of the most difficult problems United Methodism has had to face in recent years, and in each case he provided adequately the needed episcopal leadership. The first was the saving of Alaska University for its continung mission in that strategic part of the world. The second was the settlement of the famous Pacific Homes case in the Pacific Southwest Conference.

EDWARD L. TULLIS

Bishop Edward L. Tullis was elected by the 1972 Southeastern Jurisdictional Conference. At the time he was pastor of First Church, Ashland, Kentucky. An earlier pastorate was at Frankfort, the state capital. He was the first bishop to be elected from the Kentucky Conference in 118 years, the last being Bishop Hubbard H. Kavanaugh elected in 1854. Other Kentucky Conference men had received substantial votes for the episcopacy, such as the famed evangelist Dr. H. C. Morrison, but none had reached the necessary number for election. The bishop was assigned to the Columbia, South Carolina, area where he remained for eight years. In 1980 he was transferred to the Nashville area.

Prior to his election to the episcopacy, Bishop Tullis had been a popular preacher, and he continued this role in the episcopal office. There is life in his preaching, and he knows how to make the Scriptures come alive. In college he had studied under one of the truly great, but largely undiscovered, Bible teachers of the church—Dr. William E. Cassell—and much of his old teacher remained with him. No one could have studied under this teacher and remained content with less than biblical preaching. Bishop Tullis also knows the art of illustration and how to clarify the idea he is attempting to convey. His manner of deliverance is vigorous, and his messages command ready acceptance.

Bishop Tullis has a talent for administration. For three years he was an associate secretary of the Section of Church Extension of the National Division of the Board of Missions, and there he learned much that equipped him for effective administration in future years. He has the qualities of an acute businessman and is fully cognizant of financial and legal matters. The Council of Bishops discovered his knowledgeableness in this area and has called upon him for assignments where these gifts are most needed. Not the least of these was his assignment to represent the Council of Bishops in the proceedings in the Pacific Homes case.

Bishop Tullis has had a longtime interest in missions. For a number of years he served on the General Board of Missions and also led the mission activities of the Southeastern Jurisdiction. He participated in the development of Alaska Methodist University and was an active member of its board.

Evangelism has been another major interest of the bishop. He wants his churches to reach people, and he has led vigorously in programs to accomplish this end. For eight years he was a major voice in the Board of Discipleship ringing the changes in evangelism.

Still another interest has been in seeing the black minority membership accorded its full place in the church. The area which represented his first episcopal assignment had the largest ratio of black membership of any area in the church. He fell heir to developments in cross-racial progress that had already been started under his predecessor, Bishop Paul Hardin, and he carried them forward to new heights. In 1981 the General Commission on Religion and Race awarded him a special medal for the contributions which it judged him to have made to the cause of racial justice.

JOHN B. WARMAN

Bishop John B. Warman was elected by the 1972 Northeastern Jurisdictional Conference. At the time he was pastor

Additions to the Episcopal Leadership Team, 1972–1976

of Baldwin Community Church in Pittsburgh. Previously he served First Church, Pittsburgh, and had been superintendent of the Pittsburgh District. He was the fifth bishop to be elected who had a Methodist Protestant background. The others were Bishops James H. Straughn and John C. Broomfield, elected at the Uniting Conference in 1939, and Bishops Fred G. Holloway and Kenneth W. Copeland, elected in 1960. With the death of Bishop Copeland, Bishop Warman remained the only active bishop who was a former Methodist Protestant. He was assigned to the Harrisburg area to which he was returned in 1976 and again in 1980. In 1980 the Wyoming Conference was added to the area which previously had included only the Central Pennsylvania Conference.

Bishop Warman's habit has been to take a front seat in the meetings of the council and to follow closely its proceedings. Frequently, he has participated by raising a question or entering a protest. Whenever he has taken the floor, he has spoken with calmness, reason, and persuasiveness. He has been a defender of the weak, the helpless, and the exploited, and he is willing to match his words with his performance.

MELVIN E. WHEATLEY, JR.

Bishop Melvin E. Wheatley, Jr., was elected by the 1972 Western Jurisdictional Conference. At the time he was the pastor of Westwood Church, Los Angeles, where he had been pastor for eighteen years. He was originally from the Peninsula Conference. He was another of "Bishop Baker's boys" whom the bishop spotted in his seminary visitations and brought to California. He was assigned to the Denver area to which he was returned in 1976 and in 1980.

Bishop Wheatley has spoken infrequently in the Council of Bishops, but he has exhibited the capacity to move the council deeply. The bishop is a liberal who is courageous in expressing what he believes. In 1980 he took exception to a part of the Episcopal Address and at the close of the General Conference asked that his name be deleted from among the bishops' signatures. Bishop Armstrong joined him in a similar request.

Bishop Wheatley is a master preacher. He has the rare ability to take a familiar scriptural passage and make his hearers see in it something they have never seen before. He is adept at life-situation preaching and intimately relating the Bible to life today. The bishop is a master of diction, and his choice of words and sentence formation have a rare beauty. His quietness of manner in preaching adds to his effectiveness.

The bishop has chosen to major upon a pastoral administration in his area. Although his area includes the vast expanse of the states of Colorado, Wyoming, Montana, and Utah, he has managed to give it a pastoral episcopacy. He knows that an important key to progress in the life of the church is an adequate ministry, and like his mentor, Bishop Baker, he has willingly traveled long distances to find well-equipped ministers for the Denver area.

JOSEPH H. YEAKEL

Bishop Joseph H. Yeakel was elected by the 1972 Northeastern Jurisdictional Conference. At the time he was the general secretary of the General Board of Evangelism. At the time of union in 1968 two of the former Evangelical United Brethren bishops had been assigned to the Northeastern Jurisdiction and two to the North Central Jurisdiction because the largest segments of the Evangelical United Brethren Church membership were in these two jurisdictions. One each of the other Evangelical United Brethren bishops was assigned to the Western, the South Central, and the Southeastern Jurisdictions.

At the 1972 Jurisdictional Conference with Bishops Howard and Kaebnick retiring, the jurisdiction was left without an active bishop from the Evangelical United Brethren tradition. The election of Bishop Yeakel provided an active bishop with that background in the jurisdiction where so much of the former Evangelical United Brethren strength was concentrated. A second bishop out of the Evangelical United Brethren tradition came into the Northeastern College with the election of Bishop George W. Bashore in 1980. Bishop Yeakel was assigned to the Syracuse area to which he was reassigned in 1976 and in 1980. There had been another Bishop Yeakel, Reuben Yeakel, elected by the Evangelical Association in 1871. He was a distant relative.

Bishop Yeakel, elected at a young age, values his episcopal

Additions to the Episcopal Leadership Team, 1972–1976

office, but he has assumed it should carry no special privileges beyond those accorded all servants of the church. Both the Evangelical United Brethren Church and the Methodist Church had bishops, but the two churches perceived the episcopacy somewhat differently. In this regard Bishop Yeakel shares the general thinking of the tradition out of which he has come. He is democratic in spirit and seeks to operate upon a democratic pattern. He is liberal in his social views and is committed to the social as well as the personal application of the gospel. In his leadership of the Board of Evangelism he stressed the social implications of the gospel as had his predecessor once removed, Dr. Harry Denman.

Bishop Yeakel has a keen, analytical mind. Insight is one of his particular gifts. It was an enriching experience to see him stand in the council and give his studied analysis of some paper or proposal under consideration. More times than not he carried the point he was endeavoring to make.

Bishop Yeakel has been one of the best presiding officers among the bishops. He can maintain quiet command of a situation and is well versed in church and parliamentary law. The General Conference was in safe hands when he was in the chair.

BENNIE D. WARNER

Bishop Bennie D. Warner was elected by the 1973 Liberia Central Conference to succeed Bishop Stephen Nagbe, deceased. He was young, well trained, and a leader in the Liberia Conference. He regularly attended the meetings of the council, although in most cases this involved a lengthy journey for him. He took particular interest in all Central Conference affairs and was one of the Central Conference bishops most active in the council. Frequently he was called upon to give his viewpoint on affairs in the African countries.

While serving as bishop, he was elected vice-president of Liberia and took his place in the cabinet of President Tolbert. This election became a source of pride for Methodists in Liberia and for The United Methodist Church as a whole. In contrast to the action of Bishop Muzorewa in asking to be relieved of his episcopal duties while serving as prime minister of Zimbabwe, Bishop Warner took the position that he could do both jobs. He laughingly would refer to himself as being like a preacher who had been serving a station church and was now appointed to a two-point circuit.

The Council of Bishops did not challenge his contention that he could be vice-president and still attend to his responsibilities as bishop. There was no voiced disposition to raise a question at this point, and indeed if there had been, the question of whether the council had any power would have remained since the responsibility of a Central Conference bishop is finally to the Central Conference that elected him, according to the *Discipline*.

Bishop Warner's dual role was to last for only a few years, however. The Council of Bishops was in session just prior to the 1980 General Conference at Indianapolis, Indiana, and Bishop Warner and his family were present. During that meeting the shocking news came that President Tolbert and other government leaders had been assassinated and a new leadership had taken over in Liberia. Bishop Warner might have suffered the same fate had he been at home. Under the circumstances, Bishop Warner could not return to Liberia, and in 1980 the Central Conference elected Bishop Arthur F. Kulah. Bishop Warner remained in the United States and became connected with Oklahoma City University.

With his failure to be reelected, he fell into the category of "former bishops" of The United Methodist Church, along with other term bishops who for various reasons were not reelected.

J. KENNETH SHAMBLIN

Bishop J. Kenneth Shamblin was elected by the 1976 South Central Jurisdictional Conference. He was at the time pastor of St. Luke's, Houston, a pulpit he had occupied for fifteen years. Previously he had served pastorates in Arkansas and Texas and one year as district superintendent of the Searcy District. He was assigned to the New Orleans area, to which he was returned in 1980. In that year he saw the removal of the episcopal residence to Baton Rouge. As a young man Bishop Shamblin was something of a protégé of Bishop Paul Martin, who held high hopes for him but did not live to see him come into the episcopal office.

Bishop Shamblin was primarily a preacher. His messages were thoughtful, provocative, and convincing, and they were welcomed by all who heard them.

The bishop was one of the more quiet members of the council, but he keenly observed all that was happening. His great concern was the area for which he was responsible, and he gave it the same devoted and unwearied attention he had given his pastorates before he became a bishop. Bishop Shamblin died after a brief illness in 1983.

MONK BRYAN

Bishop Monk Bryan was elected by the 1976 South Central Jurisdictional Conference. At the time he was pastor of Missouri Methodist Church, Columbia, Missouri, and had served previously in the Central Texas, Missouri West, and Missouri East Conferences. He was assigned to the Nebraska area, to which he was returned in 1980.

Bishop Bryan bears the name of his grandfather, Dr. Alonzo Monk, who in his day was regarded as one of the strongest preachers of the Methodist Episcopal Church, South, and belonged in the category of the "transfer," the small company of men whom the bishops used to move from conference to conference to fill major pulpits. The bishop's father was a Methodist preacher for sixty-six years.

From 1968 to 1972 he was a member of the Structure Commission which eventually recommended radical reorganization of the board structure of the church. In all probability the proposed restructure would have been even far more radical had the commission not had on it a few persons like Dr. Bryan and Dr. Joel McDavid, both of whom were elected bishops.

Bishop Bryan is a popular preacher whose preaching is warm, enlightening, and moving. He is in great demand by his fellow bishops as a conference preacher.

The bishop is an enthusiastic participant in the Council of Bishops. Again and again he has proven to be the bishop to speak the voice of wisdom, especially in a tight and trying situation.

KENNETH W. HICKS

Bishop Kenneth W. Hicks was elected by the 1976 South Central Jurisdictional Conference. He was at the time pastor of Trinity Church, Grand Island, Nebraska. Previously he was in the Rocky Mountain Conference and had been a pastor and district superintendent in the Nebraska Conference. He was assigned to the Arkansas area to which he was reassigned in 1980.

Bishop Hicks belongs to the more liberal school, is forward in his thinking, and is committed to trying new approaches. He is a forceful exponent of the social gospel and is eager to play an active role in helping to find a Christian solution to the ills of present-day society. To this end he has given himself to study, research, observation, and the composition of occasional papers setting forth his conclusions. He gives embodiment to his convictions in his administration at the area level and in his participation in the affairs of the larger church.

Bishop Hicks found himself at the center of a whirlwind in 1982 when Arkansas became the first state to pass a law requiring public schools that teach the theory of evolution to give balanced treatment to the theory known as creation science. Bishop Hicks testified against the law. His involvement in the case was based upon theological convictions. He said, "The convictions send you right into the fray when sometimes you would rather not go."

J. CHESS LOVERN

Bishop J. Chess Lovern was elected by the 1976 South Central Jurisdictional Conference. He was at the time pastor of Boston Avenue Church, Tulsa, the same church from which his colleagues Bishops Galloway and Crutchfield had been elected previously and from which Bishop Russell would be elected in 1980. He had reached the age where he could serve only four years as an active bishop, but this did not alter the jurisdiction's choice. The bishop was assigned to the San Antonio area.

Four years earlier the South Central Jurisdiction had followed a similar course in electing Bishop Don Holter who also could serve only four years. In these two elections the South Central Jurisdiction, whether consciously or not,

Additions to the Episcopal Leadership Team, 1972–1976

contributed to providing a staggered episcopacy within the jurisdiction, thus creating a better situation than that obtaining in some other jurisdictions where as many as three-fourths of the bishops have to retire at the same time because of the proximity of their ages.

Bishop Lovern has a matter-of-fact, practical approach to administrative problems. He found his place quickly in the Council of Bishops and proved to be one of its most interesting members. The council would come to attention when he took the floor to ask a searching question or make an observation, usually cast in humorous terms.

The bishop is a unique preacher with a style all his own. His messages are filled with shrewd comments, often humorous in character, and pertinent, often homely illustrations. Frequently they contain a charming surprise element.

After four years on the San Antonio area, Bishop and Mrs. Lovern moved to Fort Worth, Texas, where the bishop assumed a connection with Texas Wesleyan.

LEROY C. HODAPP

Bishop Leroy C. Hodapp was elected by the 1976 North Central Jurisdictional Conference. At the time he was the conference council director of the South Indiana Conference. He had served as pastor and district superintendent and had been a recognized figure in Indiana Methodism for some time. He was assigned to the Illinois, area to which he was reassigned in 1980.

Bishop Hodapp is committed to progress and is willing to explore new possibilities. He feels strongly that the Council of Bishops should take a firm, positive lead in line with its historic mandate to oversee the temporal and spiritual affairs of the church.

The bishop has administrative gifts. He gave a striking example of this at the 1976 General Conference when he chaired the Committee of Chairmen. With rare skill he piloted the work of the committee to final consideration by the General Conference, always remaining calm and deliberate and refusing to be stampeded or to become confused.

Bishop Hodapp possesses an acute social conscience. He is

on the side of the poor, the exploited, and the dispossessed, and he vigorously criticizes all forms of social wrong. With his social convictions it is not surprising that in 1980 he was chosen to be the president of the Board of Church and Society.

The bishop is a clear thinker with gifts of analysis. He is able to set forth succinctly and persuasively in a well-written position paper his arguments for a particular position.

EDSEL A. AMMONS

Bishop Edsel A. Ammons was elected by the 1976 North Central Jurisdictional Conference. He was teaching at Garrett at the time. Previously he had been a minister in the African Methodist Episcopal Church but had transferred to the Rock River Conference where he served as a pastor and a member of the program staff of the conference. He was the first black to be elected by the North Central Jurisdiction, although that jurisdiction had had a black bishop in its college since 1964 in the person of Bishop James S. Thomas. Bishop Thomas had been elected by the Central Jurisdiction. Bishop Ammons was assigned to the Detroit area, to which he was reassigned in 1980.

Bishop Ammons is a clear thinker, who has the habits and approach of a scholar. He generally takes advanced positions on social questions and seeks to contribute to the coming of a new earth in which righteousness dwells. He is the defender of the rights of his own people and of other minorities. His concerns and his leadership ability were recognized by his election in 1980 as president of the General Board of Discipleship.

Bishop Ammons was marked by a great concern for the poor, and he took strong leadership in developing quiet a concern in the churches of his area. In the Council of Bishops he shared the same concern, and in 1983 drafted a thirteen-page paper entitled "A Call to the Churches on Domestic Hunger and the Economic Crisis." The paper was adopted by the Council and delivered to the entire church for study and implementation.

C. DALE WHITE

Bishop C. Dale White was elected by the 1976 Northeastern Jurisdictional Conference. At the time he was the district

Additions to the Episcopal Leadership Team, 1972–1976

superintendent of the Rhode Island-Eastern Massachusetts District. Previously he had served pastorates in Rhode Island and Massachusetts and was for seven years on the staff of the General Board of Social Concerns. He was assigned to the New Jersey area to which he was reassigned in 1980.

Bishop White is all-business, forthright in whatever he has to say. When assigned a paper in the Council of Bishops, he produced a document in which the facts were carefully marshaled and the arguments skillfully developed.

Bishop White is by nature and by choice an agent of reconciliation, and at this he is particularly adept. He is anxious to contribute to the resolution of conflict, and he knows something of that art. The most striking example of this was his dramatic leadership prior to, during, and after the time of the 1980 General Conference in the effort to help resolve the Iranian hostage crisis. This story promises to be told again and again for years to come.

NGOY KIMBA WAKADILO

Bishop Ngoy Kimba Wakadilo was elected by the 1976 Africa Central Conference. He was elected from the directorship of Mulangwishi Theological School. At that time the work in Zaire had grown to the extent that establishment of a second episcopal area appeared desirable. The North Shaba area was established, and he was assigned to it. He was reelected in 1980 for life, and the same area assignment was renewed.

Bishop Wakadilo has attended the Council of Bishops with fair regularity and has been a silent, patient member of the group. His primary interest is the developing work in his own area and the growth of the church in Africa.

ALMEIDA PENICELA

Bishop Almeida Penicela was elected by the 1976 Africa Central Conference. He was assigned to the Mozambique area. Previously he had been a pastor and a teacher. Immediately after his election, he was so severely injured in an automobile accident that his life was despaired of. In time he recovered, however, but was confined to a wheelchair. Thus handicapped, he administered his area and attended the General Conference at Indianapolis. In 1980 he was reelected.

LAVERNE D. MERCADO

Bishop LaVerne D. Mercado was elected by the 1976 Philippines Central Conference.

Within a matter of only a few months he felt compelled to resign because of ill health, and Bishop Granadosin was forced once again to carry the load of the entire work in the Philippines for the balance of the quadrennium.

HERMANN L. STICHER

Bishop Hermann L. Sticher was elected by the 1977 Germany Central Conference. He had been a pastor and district superintendent in the South Germany Conference. He was a minister in the former Evangelical United Brethren Church in Germany prior to union in 1968, having been ordained by Bishop George Epp. He is the only native German coming out of the Evangelical United Brethren constituency in that land to be elected to the episcopacy during the twenty-two years of the existence of the Evangelical United Brethren Church (1946–1968) and the subsequent years of the life of The United Methodist Church.

Bishop Sticher is scholarly, matter-of-fact, efficient, and well informed on current developments in church and state. He is bilingual and speaks English as easily as German. His area consists of three Annual Conferences in West Germany.

SHANTU K. PARMAR

Bishop Shantu K. Parmar was elected by the 1979 Southern Asia Central Conference. He was at the time educational secretary of the Central Conference and previously had taught in Leonard Theological Seminary. He was assigned to the Bombay area. He was the last of the bishops elected by the Southern Asia Central Conference, and his service as a United Methodist bishop was confined to little more than a year, since the church in India became autonomous in 1980. In the new church he was assigned to the Lucknow area.

VIII
EXERCISING A GROUP LEADERSHIP ROLE TODAY

United Methodism expects each of its bishops to play a personal leadership role at the level of the area to which he or she is assigned, but beyond that it also expects the bishops as a body to play a collective leadership role.

The traditional Methodist terminology for the episcopacy was "the itinerant general superintendency," and its continuing time-honored mandate to its bishops has been "to travel throughout the connection." The episcopacy of United Methodism has been and continues to be, therefore, a general superintendency of the church.

When William McKendree was elected in 1808, Bishop Asbury, with Bishop Coke so largely absent from the country, had functioned as the sole active bishop of the church for twenty-four years with the exception of the six years he had the company of Bishop Whatcoat. He wrote, "They elected Brother McKendree assistant bishop." McKendree, in effect by the position he took, said, "Who said so?" and the church agreed. Since that long ago day, Methodism has held strongly to the parity of its episcopacy, and the bishops together have been expected to exercise a general superintendency.

At first, the bishops of Methodism (only two in number) exercised this general superintendency by traveling together to all the Annual Conferences. Later when they became three in number, they divided the Annual Conference sessions among them each year. For long years they annually made a plan of episcopal visitation, normally assigning different conferences to each bishop each year, thus assuring a general superintendency of the church.

Even after the area system was adopted by the Methodist

Episcopal Church, provision was made for one session of each conference per quadrennium to be held by some bishop other than the bishop assigned to the area, again a concession to the concept of a general superintendnecy. During the first few years after Methodist union in 1939, it was customary for the council upon request of the area bishop to appoint some other bishop to hold a particular conference session, but this custom was abandoned years ago.

Another symbol of the parity of bishops to which Methodism has long held was the plan once followed by the bishops of the Methodist Episcopal Church; all the bishops would preside in rotation at sessions of the Board of Bishops according to the order of their election. Thus, at one meeting perhaps as many as ten or twelve bishops would occupy the chair, and where the rotation left off, it would be picked up again at the next meeting.

A similar symbol of the parity of bishops was the custom in the Methodist Episcopal Church, South, of having the bishops preside in rotation by seniority in the General Conference. This sometimes resulted in having the wrong bishop in the chair when the parliamentary situation demanded certain skills. Parity of the episcopacy means that all bishops have the same authority and functions, the same privilege of attending the meetings, and the same vote in the Council of Bishops as long as they remain on the active list.

None of the churches now composing The United Methodist Church have ever been willing to accord to one bishop a status not accorded to all. Certain bishops, such as Matthew Simpson, William C. Harris, Warren A. Candler, John M. Moore, and G. Bromley Oxnam, have played almost dominating roles among the council members, but it has been because of the strength of their personalities and their ability rather than by assignment.

Since 1939 the Council of Bishops has followed the rule of having a bishop serve as president of the Council for only one year and not being subject to reelection, again suggesting the parity of the episcopacy by providing that the honor of the presidency shall be distributed among the bishops as widely as possible.

Exercising a Group Leadership Role Today

In the General Conference of 1966, Dr. Robert Cushman presented a floor amendment that would have provided for a "presiding bishop," but after some discussion the amendment was voted down. In the 1968 conference the Council of Bishops itself proposed something much milder. As a result of the only ballot vote on a motion in the council within the memory of even some of the oldest bishops, by a margin of 48 to 14 the council suggested constitutional legislative changes that would have allowed one bishop to be released from area responsibility to serve as full-time secretary of the Council of Bishops. The proposal received the necessary vote in the General Conference and the Annual Conferences, but the technicality was raised in the 1970 conference that the 1968 conference was a uniting conference, not a General Conference. Therefore a second vote was taken. In this case the proposal failed to receive the necessary majority, and the matter became closed. The explanation of the failure seems to be that United Methodism is afraid of entrusting a status to any one bishop that it does not accord to all. It would appear that it remains committed to a general superintendencey of the church by the full body of bishops.

A general superintendency requires by its very nature a collective exercise of leadership by the Council of Bishops. This is no easy or simple assignment, for the council faces problems today that have not had to be faced before.

There is first of all the growing size of the council. Today it is slightly more than 40 percent larger than it was twenty-five years ago. This has come as a result of changes in the basic number of bishops allowed each jurisdiction, a lower retirement age, union with the Evangelical United Brethren Church, and the increase in the number of bishops authorized to be elected by Central Conferences. The Committee on Administrative Concerns today has a larger membership than the total Board of Bishops of the Methodist Episcopal Church at the time of union.

Another problem for the exercising of collective leadership by the council today grows out of the present diversity of the church. United Methodism is a world church, and with modern means of travel it can operate as such without distance representing the difficulty it once did. The churches overseas from the United States represent other cultures and concerns, and in the exercise of its collective leadership the council must now consider a world rather than a largely localized agenda.

A further problem for exercising collective leadership by the council grows out of the need for research and the necessity for someone to be able to devote the time demanded for adequate consideration of propositions. Each member of the council already has upon him or her the demands of an area, including the secretary whose responsibility it is largely to keep the council going. Individual members occasionally somehow find time to contribute to some particular consideration, but there has been no central resource bank to which to turn and no individual available to do the spadework for which effective collective leadership often has to call.

Collective leadership upon the part of the Council of Bishops must include both a pastoral and a prophetic role. One of the functions of the Council of Bishops is the pastoral role of holding the church together. United Methodism is a widely diversified and pluralistic church. It is made up of all kinds of people, representing many shades of opinion and many loyalties in addition to their loyalty to United Methodism. Sometimes tensions arise in the church that are severe in character. Then the bishops have a pastoral role to play in helping the people of the church to understand each other, to hear each other, to resolve to love while differing, and to bridge their diversity by way of their ultimate loyalty to the One who is forever the head of the church and the Lord of all.

The long story of United Methodism includes numerous faithful attempts upon the part of the episcopacy to hold the church together. This is illustrated by the ill-fated attempt of the bishops in 1844 to prevent the division of the church; by the efforts of the bishops of both the Methodist Episcopal Church and the Methodist Episcopal Church, South, and the president of the Methodist Protestant Church to carry each church intact into the union; and by the leadership of the Evangelical United Brethren Church bishops in seeking to make a success of the union of 1968.

Exercising a Group Leadership Role Today

Not only in times of decision or strain do the bishops serve to hold the church together but also in the discharge of their ongoing responsibility. The Council of Bishops is in effect the cement that binds the church together. General Conferences meet, transact their business, and adjourn, and their membership changes largely each quadrennium. Boards and agencies help the church carry forward its mission, but each is confined to a particular area of responsibility. But in the Council of Bishops every church and every individual Methodist anywhere in the world have an advocate at court and every cause some friend. Moreover, the Council of Bishops serves as a continuing bond of unity between the church of yesterday and the church of today. The time span between the episcopal service years of its present oldest members and its youngest members represents a period of approximately a half century.

The bishops of the church in the exercise of their pastoral role act upon the assumption that the church as an institution may be an instrument as well as an instittuion and that therefore it is eminently worth saving.

The Council of Bishops has, however, more than just a collective pastoral role to play. It is called to play a prophetic role, being critical where criticism is needed, speaking a "Thus saith the Lord" regarding all wrong in personal or social life, demanding that all things be made "according to the pattern shown thee on the mount," and calling the church to claim all of life for the lordship of Christ.

The Council of Bishops seeks to exercise the collective leadership to which it is called, first of all, through its semiannual meetings. There it addresses itself to the state of the church and what needs to be done about it. It considers various problems that relate to the church's life and mission and lifts up for the attention of the people of the church subjects and causes that merit their attention and response. It remembers that the church in every hour lives its life against the backdrop of current history and that it is and must be involved in all that is happening in society. The council therefore from time to time suggests guidelines to the membership of the church for the consideration of some pressing social problem in the light of the demands of the gospel. On occasion it also expresses to the public its convictions on some pressing issue through a statement of position released to the press. Also it conveys to executives, legislators, and community leaders its thinking as to what social righteousness demands in particular situations.

The Council of Bishops is currently organized with a view toward discharging such pastoral and prophetic leadership responsibilities. The council functions primarily through four committees to one of which every bishop, active or retired, is assigned. The committees are (1) Administrative Concerns, (2) Pastoral Concerns, (3) Teaching Concerns, and (4) Relational Concerns. Matters requiring attention are first referred to one of the committees, there matured, and recommendations reported back to the full council. The council regularly examines its own pattern of operation and is committed to adjustment should such appear to be best for the welfare of the church.

The Council of Bishops, when the occasion seems to demand, issues a message to the church. Quadrennially it speaks to the church through the time-honored Episcopal Address to the General Conference. Its recommendations by courtesy motion of some delegate become a part of the agenda of the various committees of the General Conference.

The Council of Bishops thus seeks to function as an assembly of "general superintendents." Whatever the council decides is channeled down to the Annual Conferences through the active bishops and from there with the help of the district superintendents to each church in the connection.

United Methodism continues to call for effective collective episcopal leadership for the church. If such a desire is to be realized, the church must do at least two things. First of all, it must elect men and women to the episcopacy who have demonstrated leadership potential. And then, having elected them, it must see that the legislation of the church affecting the episcopacy leaves the way open for an effective leadership role to be played.